SWEENEY TODD

The True Story of The Demon Barber of Fleet Street

SWEENEY TODD

The True Story of
The Demon Barber of Fleet Street

Peter Haining

ROBSON
BOOKS

First published in hardback in 1993 by Robson Books.
First paperback edition published in 2002 by Robson Books.

This updated edition published in Great Britain in 2007 by
Robson Books
10 Southcombe Street
London
W14 0RA

An imprint of Anova Books Company Ltd

ISBN 9781861059895

A CIP catalogue record for this book is available from the British Library.

10 9 8 7 6 5 4 3 2 1

Printed and bound by Cromwell Press, Trowbridge, Wiltshire (England).
Typeset by SX Composing DTP, Rayleigh, Essex

This book can be ordered direct from the publisher.
Contact the marketing department, but try your bookshop first.

www.anovabooks.com

'Sweeney Todd the barber was a sporty sort of man,
He profiteered in razors on the very latest plan
The trap he set for customers was Sweeney's little joke;
When the buyer found the cellar, the cellar found him broke,
But Sweeney Todd's successors have found a better line,
And the body in the cellar is the body in the wine.'

G.K. Chesterton (1874-1936)

'Sweeney Todd will never die. We all need bogeymen
and he was bogier than most.'

Anna Pavord, *Observer,* 29 January, 1979

Author's Note

When the first edition of this book was published over a decade ago in 1993 there was still much in dispute about the life of Sweeney Todd, the Nineteenth Century serial killer. Subsequent research during the ensuing years – as well as a number of important historical discoveries – have, I believe, now established his existence beyond doubt. This extensively revised and rewritten account at last reveals the full story of the Demon Barber of Fleet Street – and of the legend that has made him an icon in criminal history.

PETER HAINING
September, 2007

CONTENTS

A Dreadful Tale of Crime

The lowering grey clouds over London had been causing a fine drizzle ever since dawn and were now growing heavier with the possibility of a storm as evening drew in. The close press of buildings around Temple Bar were running with water and in the streets the usual fetid puddles were growing bigger, forcing pedestrians to step aside nimbly to avoid the spray caused by any horse drawn vehicle that laboured by. There were, in fact, fewer people about than usual in Fleet Street and those who were, pressed themselves up as close as they could to the buildings to escape from the worst of the weather.

There was still a touch of winter in the air, although it was well into the month of March, and although it was not quite five o'clock, the general gloom of the day made it seem like night already. Flickering candles were visible through the windows of most of the shops and taverns and it was only when a door was suddenly opened by a customer going in or out that any flash of colour and warmth spilled into the grim roadway outside.

In the general murkiness, the street seemed almost timeless: the outlines of the buildings indistinct in the half-light, with the people huddled shapelessly into their clothes as they hurried by. At this moment in time, the road was free of traffic and even the few street sellers who usually peddled their wares had disappeared into the alleyways or taverns. There seemed to be an air of depression abroad.

The year was 1785, the fifteenth year of the reign of George III. To all intents and purposes it was a year very like any other of late; and Fleet Street was continuing to be the place where the curious came to gawp at the sights and the exhibitions ranged along its length. But both the date and place were destined soon to find a lasting place in the history of the metropolis because of the particular activities of a man who lived and practised his profession there. A man who history would for years claim never existed at all . . .

A lone figure wrapped up well in an expensive dark cloak with his gold-braided three-cornered hat pulled down over his eyes, paused just before he reached the huge bulk of St Dunstan's Church. A whirring sound had caught his attention above the spattering drops of rain. His eyes went up to the big clock projecting from the side of the church. The man saw from the large, ornate hands that the hour was just about to strike.

For a moment there was stillness: and then two small doors opened beside the clock face. A pair of gold painted figures representing savages, each armed with a club, slowly emerged, their heads moving rhythmically from side to side. With mechanical efficiency they alternately struck five blows on the two bells suspended between them. Then as smoothly as they had appeared, the figures disappeared back into the alcove.

Ignoring the rain which dripped onto his face, the man watched in delight the performance of the 'Giants of St Dunstan's,' which, on a fine day, would draw sightseers and visitors to London like himself and halt the flow of pedestrians. Even standing on his own in the drizzle, the sight was still something to engage the senses of a man visiting London for the first time.

The stranger smiled to himself. The sight had pleased him. Indeed, the whole day was giving him pleasure, despite the bad weather. What with his successful business transaction that morning and now the time to look around the city before he sought a bed for the night prior to going home the next day, he had reason to feel satisfied with his visit. The money that was folded in his wallet was an extra delight, too.

A few moments more and the man then turned his attention away from the church towards the stylish archway of Temple Bar just ahead spanning the road. The gates were open and lights burned brightly in the little windows on either side. The edifice seemed to rear up against the darkening sky. But it was not frightening, he thought, rather more majestic, a kind of symbol of the power and authority of his nation's great capital. He was just about to walk on towards it, when something else caught his attention out of the corner of his eye.

He turned slightly and found he was outside a barber's shop. What had caught his eye had been the flash of something silver in the candlelight. A flash that repeated itself, once, twice and then was gone. The shop was rather dark and unattractive looking: the overhanging gables throwing everything beneath into even darker shadows. The main window was dirt-encrusted and a solitary notice that hung in the lea of a barber's striped pole was almost illegible through the grime:

'*Easy Shaving for a Penny – As Good as You Will Find Any.*'

The quaint expression caused another grin to spread across the man's face. He looked above the window and there read a legend in fat, yellow letters: 'SWEENEY TODD, BARBER.' Almost unconsciously, he ran one hand over his damp chin and throat. His beard was already rough to the touch. It had been the very early hours of the morning when he had set out from his home just across the River Thames and he had been so anxious not to be late for his appointment he knew that his shave had not been very thorough.

Now that he was going to stay in the city for the night, perhaps he had better smarten himself up? After all, he was quite well off for the moment, and who knew what the night might bring? He could well afford a shave and some good barbering. And perhaps the shop was not so bad on the inside? Yes, he decided, he would go in and experience Mr Todd's tonsorial skills. The stranger pushed open the door and walked inside.

The man had no way of knowing that it would be the very last door he would ever open . . . or close.

* * *

In July 1980 when Stephen Sondheim's Emmy award-winning 'Musical Thriller', *Sweeney Todd,* opened in London, a considerable amount of the original research that I had been gathering for years about the Demon Barber of Fleet Street was used as the basis for a TV Special on Melvyn Bragg's *South Bank Show* which discussed the making and shaping of the stage production. At the same time I was also asked to contribute an introduction to a new edition of one of the classic melodramas about the cut-throat barber written in 1862 by the Victorian playwright Frederick Hazellton.

There was still, at that time, a great deal of confusion and disagreement about Sweeney Todd, which I went to some lengths to describe. In particular, whether the man had really existed at all, or was simply the product of an author's fertile imagination. It was a question that had fascinated me for twenty years ever since my early career as a journalist employed in Fleet Street – and one I was still very keen to answer.

As a result of my involvement in that television programme – which, incidentally, also won an Emmy award for London Weekend Television in the performing arts category – not to mention the republication of the Victorian melodrama, I received a number of interesting letters and communications from people similarly intrigued by the mystery surrounding the Demon Barber. These missives spoke of old manuscripts in the British Museum, documents held in the Guildhall in London, and a number of eighteenth- and nineteenth-century journals and newspapers on file in the British Library at Colindale. There were hints, too, that the Library of Congress in Washington D.C. also had some interesting data relating to Sweeney Todd.

Because of the pressure of other commitments, I was not free to follow all these leads immediately. But in the intervening years I have, one by one, followed up each of the suggestions – travelling to Washington as well as combing London in the search – and I have discovered new and invaluable information to supplement what was already in my possession. These clues pointed inescapably to the fact that Sweeney Todd *had* existed and that his life and crimes were more intriguing, more curious and, if anything, more gruesome than had previously been suspected.

It was certainly also impossible to escape from the conclusion that much of Sweeney Todd's notoriety had stemmed directly from a Victorian 'Penny Dreadful' serial which had subsequently been pirated for use in plays at the cheap London theatres during the closing years of Queen Victoria's reign. But equally certainly beneath this fiction there lay a substrata of fact that no amount of romanticising could hide. The belief expressed by some historians that the Demon Barber was a composite figure made from other serial killers was certainly tenable; but the facts that I came across in those manuscripts, documents and newspapers produced enough concrete evidence to enable me to recreate the life of this man whose cut-throat killings have caused him to be described as 'the greatest mass murderer in English history'.

It was a story made all the more fascinating because of two extraordinary elements unlike any others to be found in criminal history. Firstly, there was Sweeney Todd's use of a revolving shaving chair to trap his victims; and, secondly, the fact that he had a partner-in-crime, a woman, who helped in disposing of the bodies by turning the flesh into meat pies.

In writing this full story of Sweeney Todd, I have had access not only to all the evidence already mentioned, but in addition the opportunity to study the various well-known novelisations and serialisations of his life that have appeared over the years since the mid-1800s. From their pages I have similarly been able to sift more facts from amidst the fiction, with the result that while clearly separating one from the other, I am at last able to write what I believe is the true story of the Demon Barber.

The facts about Sweeney Todd's life are made all the more fascinating by what was happening in London during the later part of the eighteenth century: the depradation and poverty of the people; the general lawlessness, drunkenness and crime in which they lived; and the gradual emergence of acceptable working conditions, literacy and social order. These were the elements which initially enabled a mass killer like Todd to survive, but as they changed brought about his downfall. This is a story as much about society and its mores as the horrific crimes of one man.

At the end of my search for Sweeney Todd one question still remained to be answered. *Why* should we have been fascinated for so long by a man who was, to all intents and purposes, a callous murderer with no qualms about cannibalism? A forerunner, it would appear, to the cinema's number one human monster today, Hannibal Lector? The history books indicate that the public has always had a morbid interest in this theme, and psychologists have pointed out that one of mankind's most persistent subconscious fears is that of being killed and eaten. Sweeney Todd indeed epitomises that feeling one gets when eating a meat pie about just what *might* have gone into its manufacture; and the strange, tingling apprehension which creeps over anyone who leans back in a hairdresser's chair and waits for the razor or the scissors to be applied to the hairs on the neck or throat.

Reay Tannahill in her fascinating book, *Flesh and Blood: A History of the Cannibal Complex* (1975), says that many of the old beliefs about flesh, blood and the spirit are still buried somewhere in the recesses of our minds, but the public expression of them has become almost jaundiced. 'Except when it really happens,' she says, 'eating people is no longer startling or even very remarkable, just blackly humorous.' Miss Tannahill then goes on to cite a story which proves – if proof is needed – that the Sweeney Todd story will probably remain with us always.

Apparently not very long ago there was a group of people in London distributing leaflets which warned against the activities of a 'world-wide neo-Nazi apparatus' which was said to be set on removing up to eight million British citizens. No reason was given for this or even how those who had been selected would be eliminated. Some of the victims, the leaflet declared, had already been disposed of and their bodies made into various innocuous items which had been slipped into the merchandising system. The items were leather goods, soap powder, fertiliser and – yes, you have already guessed – *meat pies*!

The public interest in the legend of Sweeney Todd seems to me never to have been in doubt. Perhaps the most unusual example of this happened only a short while ago in November 1991. A special production of Sondheim's musical was being mounted in Wormwood Scrubs, the London prison which houses a considerable number of murderers serving life sentences. Several of the inmates were playing roles in the musical, although the leading roles were being sung by professionals from the Pimlico Opera Company who had been invited to stage the production.

'What will people make of it?' one inmate was reported to have asked a member of the opera company. 'A bunch of murderers doing an opera about a bunch of murderers?' It was not a question that anyone felt qualified to answer. Indeed, probably only Sweeney Todd himself could have provided one. But then he would surely have found it the most curious twist of all in the legend which surrounds his name – that after all these years the story had finally came back full circle to prison where it had all begun.

The Legend of the Demon Barber

The name Sweeney Todd, the notorious Demon Barber of Fleet Street with his famous catch-phrase, 'I polish 'em off,' is one of the most famous as well as enigmatic in the annals of crime. Renowned in folklore, sensational fiction, plays, films and, most recently, a lavish stage musical, he enjoys a world-wide notoriety as one of the earliest serial killers who perpetrated crimes that were as ingenious in their execution as they were ghoulish in their *modus operandi*.

His name is, in fact, one that hardly needs any introduction. To generations of children he has been held up as a razor-wielding bogeyman who would cut them up and make them into meat pies – long before Freddy Krueger became a nightmare in today's Elm Street movies, slashing children to death with razor-sharp fingers. To the older generation, Todd has also been regarded as a blood-soaked villain who cunningly used a revolving chair in his shop to tumble victims into a deep cellar below. Here, their throats were cut and any valuables removed, before the corpses were taken through underground passageways to his accomplice-in-crime, a pastrycook named Mrs Lovett, who turned them into pies for sale in her shop. The elements of cold-blooded murder and cannibalism made the story at once electrifying and appalling in the extreme.

These basic details of the story of Sweeney Todd are, in fact, as familiar in London lore as those of Jack the Ripper or Doctor Cnppen; while his place in the history of crime in the city is as assured as that of Guy Fawkes or Dick Turpin. And although Fleet Street, where he carried out his hideous crimes in an unprepossessing little shop, has changed out of all recognition in the intervening two centuries since they were perpetrated, his ghost still haunts the former 'Street of Ink' and attracts curiosity seekers from all over the world. Unfortunately, no trace of that shop at 186 Fleet Street – or the other one occupied by Mrs Lovett in Bell Yard – still exists, but his reputation remains undiminished: if anything, it has become further enhanced. Indeed, in a grim little twist of fate, his name has even become synonymous in Cockney rhyming slang with those officers of the law bent on catching arch-criminals like him – the 'Sweeney' (Todd) or Flying Squad.

Yet for all his fame, the facts about Sweeney Todd's crimes remain remarkably poorly documented. Certainly, though, there are numerous references to him in case histories of crime as well as books about London.

In *The Crimes of London* by H. W. Maskell (1876), for instance, Todd is referred to as 'the most dastardly criminal of the age'. Maskell relates how when Todd was finally arrested, his premises were 'found crammed with property and clothing sufficient for 160 people'. *One hundred and sixty people!* – exaggerated or not, this total surely immediately places the Demon Barber among the forefront of the greatest mass-murderers in English history.

Charles Dickens, who began writing in the early part of the Eighteenth Century, certainly knew all about the Demon Barber and mentions him in his novel, *Martin Chuzzlewit*, published in 1844. At the time he was writing this story, the figure of the demon barber had not yet been established by theatre melodramas and serial stories as a central part of Victorian lore. But Dickens may well have known about the tradition on which Todd was based and certainly, like many of his contemporaries, indulged himself in melodrama in all its forms. Aside from leaving us a vivid picture of a night of 'Blood and Thunder' at a London theatre in *The Uncommercial Traveller* (1861), he also has this to say about his reading habits:

'I used, when I was at school, to take in the *Terrific Register,* making myself unspeakably miserable and frightening my very wits out of my head, for the small charge of a penny weekly; which, considering that there was an illustration to every number, in which there was always a pool of blood, and at least one body, was cheap.'

The Sweeney Todd undertones in *Martin Chuzzlewit,* should the reader need reminding, are to be found at the end of Chapter 36:

"'Upon my word," thought Tom [Pinch], quickening his pace, "I don't know what John will think has become of me. He'll begin to be afraid I have strayed into one of those streets where the countrymen are murdered; and that I have been made meat pies of, or some such horrible thing."'

The theme also surfaces again in the next chapter: 'Tom's evil genius did not lead him into the dens of any of those preparers of cannibalistic pastry who are represented in many standard country legends as doing a lively retail business in the Metropolis.'

Although these are clearly references to Sweeney Todd, Dickens may well have refrained from being more specific because of the possibility that some among his readers might have lost friends or relatives in the infamous barber's shop a little over forty years earlier.

William Kent in his interesting chronicle, *London Mystery and Mythology* (1952), mentions several old residents of the capital city who had told him stories about Sweeney Todd.

'Sir William Treloar, who was born over the famous carpet shop on Ludgate Hill, was familiar with the story of the Demon Barber and held it to be true. He also used to tell how, with a group of playfellows, he delighted in going into a barber's shop which stood at the corner of Fleet Street and Fetter Lane, with a doorway in each. At a concerted signal they would rush through the front door one after another and, shouting "Sweeney Todd" as they went, dash out of the Fetter Lane door. There was a rush as the last one ran a risk of being caught.'

Another writer, Clement Scott, a Victorian critic who was involved with the London theatre scene throughout the second half of the nineteenth century, adds to this statement in his memoirs, *The Drama of Yesterday* (1899):

'Old Temple Bar and its neighbourhood up to that day I always loved, although George Augustus Sala was forever telling us that the gate was not old at all. Within the fabric of Old Temple Bar was a tiny barber's shop where I have often been shaved. The Figaro who presided over the establishment delighted in tilting up the chair of his customers, and as the City boundaries came right through the shop he said, "Now you are in the West End – now you are in the City!"'

'I resented this joke, for I always thought of that grim drama by George Dibdin Pitt, first performed at the Brittania, Hoxton and called *Sweeney Todd, The Barber of Fleet Street; or The String of Pearls*. Sweeney Todd used to leave his customers sitting in the shaving chair on some paltry excuse, whereupon chair, customer and valuables disappeared through a trap to the cellar below, where the customer was robbed and promptly murdered. I always connected that shop with Sweeney Todd; in fact I do so to this day.'

And just to underline these recollections, we have H. G. Hibbert, another historian of the stage, writing in his *A Playgoer's Memories* (1920):

'When I was a young Londoner I was shown in Fleet Street the very shop of the Demon Barber – and shuddered to think that meat pies were still on sale there. I read that an enterprising tradesman has again, by way of advertisement, labelled the new building erected on its site as the authentic abode of the wretch. I think it quite conceivable that there was a scoundrel, deep-dyed as the ghastly Todd, in the dark, Georgian days of London.'

Nor should it be inferred from these examples that the belief in Sweeney Todd was confined to journalists, men of the theatre and children. For in 1878 during one of the periodic outbursts of interest into his origins, a correspondent signing himself 'S.P.' and writing most appropriately from Temple, London provided some interesting remarks for readers of the fascinating miscellany of facts, *Notes & Queries*. Under the heading, 'An Old Cockney Tradition,' in the issue of 21 September 1878, he reported:

'The story was asserted to be founded upon a veritable tragedy enacted in London in the eighteenth century – the age of clean shaving and cheap mutton pies. Sweeney Todd (there is a circumstantiality, so to speak, about the name which induces a belief in a fact as the foundation for the tradition) was a barber carrying on his business in Fleet Street in one of two adjoining houses owned by him. In the other dwelling his wife made and sold mutton pies. The gist of the legend may be gathered from the combined assertions that the barber's customers were never seen to emerge from the shaving establishment and that his wife, the pie-maker, was never known to purchase mutton. I happen to know, from my own personal experience, that the lower classes of London believed in the substantial truth of this story. I can trace this credulity back (by report, of course) for at least seventy years. It is never recounted without the addition that the shaver was at last detected, convicted and suffered at Tyburn.'

All of these writers shared the view that Sweeney Todd's shop had stood close to Temple Bar the former 'Gateway to the City of London' as it was known. Historian Walter George Bell in his magisterial study, *Fleet Street in Seven Centuries* (1912) is more specific:

'The barber, keeping shop near St Dunstan's, enticed customers to his fatal chair. It rested over a trap-door, by means whereof the half-shaved, unsuspecting victim was dropped into the cellar and there despatched. He reappeared only in the pastry vended by the next door pieman [sic]. It is a fact that one of the two gabled houses in Fleet Street between Fetter Lane and St Dunstan's Church, was long occupied as a pie-shop, where business appears to have flourished despite the gruesome association.'

Several writers also reported having heard stories about a pie shop supposed to have existed in Bell Yard at this same point in history and perhaps linked to the barber's premises by interconnecting tunnels.

'There are plenty of underground apartments in Fleet Street,' William Kent added in his narrative. 'Beneath the Cheshire Cheese Tavern are vaults so extensive that they have been assigned by some to a religious priory.'

Another writer, Thomas Nelson, referring to Sweeney Todd by the nickname ascribed to him by Victorian Londoners as 'Old Cut 'em Up', said in his book, *Memories of Old London* (1904), that in the city the barber was held to be 'the worst of the worst' with a record of crimes 'unmatched for their coldblooded, hardened and pitiless criminality'.

Alan Dent, for years the distinguished theatre critic of the *Guardian,* and a man who had a particular interest in the stage melo-dramas about Sweeney Todd, had this to say in an article he wrote specially for *Lilliput* magazine in 1942: 'The legend has been in existence since the days of George III and the experts agree that it probably has a basis in fact. Fouche's *Archives of the Police* have an account of a similar series of murders in Paris, the victims being "polished off" in a barber's shop and then made into pies which were sold for human consumption.

'The Fleet Street tradition was in existence long before this, however. The late Chance Newton, who saw many of the early versions of the melodrama, investigated the matter carefully and came to the conclusion that Todd's shop was close to St Dunstan's-in-the-West at the highest point of Fleet Street. Until the year 1913 the site was occupied by Craig's celebrated fish restaurant. The sinister pie shop was situated in Bell Yard.

'Topographically, this is a little awkward, since it sets the barber's and the pie shop improbably far apart. However, the cellar where the chopping and baking were done was "of vast extent and sepulchral appearance". It must have extended right under Chancery Lane and what is now the Law Courts branch of the Bank of England.'

Alongside these references, however, there are others which assert that the man was nothing more than a figment of the imagination; that no such barber ever existed outside the pages of fiction or the repertory theatres. In July 1980, for example the *Sunday Times* theatre critic Bevis Hillier completely refuted his predecessor's remarks by declaring, 'Almost certainly no demon barber called Sweeney Todd ever existed; but there is cut-throat competition over the identity of the real-life figure (or figures) on whom he was based.' (The careful use of the word 'almost' will probably strike the reader as strongly as it did me!)

In truth, the tale of the Demon Barber is one of the most bloodthirsty and intriguing to be found anywhere in the world, compounded by the lack of research and precious few documents on which to draw. It is a story that has fascinated me ever since the early days of my career in journalism when I worked for several years in Fleet Street at a time when it was still the newspaper centre of Britain.

Here, ostensibly just a stone's throw from the scene of his crimes, I kept running across versions of the Demon Barber's activities and conflicting stories about his reality. His name was one that cropped up with maddening frequency in discussions held in the Fleet Street pubs and was heard from tourists in the street asking for directions to 'where Sweeney Todd's shop was supposed to be'.

As a result I spent many fascinating hours walking the part of Fleet Street where he lived, visiting the shop at number 186 where he allegedly practised his barbering and cut his victims' throats (now completely rebuilt and occupied by an office equipment supplier), and strolling through quiet Bell Yard nearby, where Mrs Lovett's pie shop was said to be located.

I also examined the interior of the handsome St Dunstan's Church at the Strand end of Fleet Street, underneath which the passageway used for moving the corpses was said to run. I tried to picture in my mind's eye what the imposing gate of Temple Bar which had stood adjacent to the church looked like before it was removed and the spot marked by the present Griffin memorial.

I pored over old records of Fleet Street and its inhabitants, looked at eighteenth-century maps for evidence of the actual premises used by

Todd and Mrs Lovett, and carefully studied old engravings of the area in the hope I might spot a tiny shop bearing the legend, 'Sweeney Todd, Barber' or even just 'Barber'.

As time passed, the site took on the same sense of mystery for me that is associated with Whitechapel and the haunts of Jack the Ripper. Here was another area that was famous for a murderer both notorious and enigmatic. The similarities between the two men were curious, too: for just as the identity of Jack the Ripper has evaded the attentions of numerous writers and researchers, so Sweeney Todd has remained, through all the years since his death, a figure shrouded in conjecture. Both, though, have left their bloody and indelible mark across the fabric of London history.

As I walked through the area of Fleet Street on many a warm summer's day – and then again on dark winter evenings – the burning question of his reality kept returning to my thoughts. Every time I passed the Royal Courts of Justice I was reminded just how remarkable it was that such a legend could have grown up in the very shadow of this great centre of British justice – and yet there still remained in the minds of people this doubt as to whether it had happened at all.

I was also surprised to find that for all his notoriety, there was no full length biography of the Demon Barber. There had been articles and features in magazines and newspapers, to be sure; but, despite the continuing growth of his fame in all areas of the media, the full story of Sweeney Todd still remained to be written.

And so, over the intervening years, I have painstakingly combed the fact and fiction to produce what I believe to be the full story. I began, naturally enough, by looking at the earlier accounts of murderous barbers which some believed might have been the model for Sweeney Todd. They proved to be interesting, if grisly, reading.

Who Was The Real Sweeney Todd?

The earliest of all the stories that have been claimed to be the inspiration for the legend of the Demon Barber of Fleet Street dates from as far back as the fifteenth century and takes the form of a medieval ballad written in French. The ballad was apparently sung by Parisian mothers as a warning to recalcitrant offspring. Later, it was adapted by folk singers and sung with relish to the tune of *Lejeune Homme Emoisonne* – 'The Young Man Who Was Poisoned'. The words are as follows:

> *Towards the end of the Fourteenth Century*
> *There lived a sort of Demon Barber,*
> *Who slit his clients throats at 24 Rue des Marmouzets.*

> *He carried on this horrible trade*
> *And nobody could resist him,*
> *In his cellar he polished them off*
> *His accomplice a villainous pie merchant next door.*

> *CHORUS: With a pie – with a mer – with a chant,*
> *With a pie – mer – chant. Ha! Ha!*

> *This horrid tale also tells us*
> *That he worked with a ferocious female*
> *Fiercer than the fiercest bailiff.*

> *For all the poor devils he killed*
> *His partner converted into pork pies!*

And he said of his customers when defunct,
They are gone – pork creatures!

CHORUS: With a pork – with a cre – with a ture
With a pork creature. Ha! Ha!

In a book of old French Ballads published in 1845 where I found a copy of these verses, the editor, M. Lurine, commented that 300 years later the story was still being told to young listeners – and for many of them 'nothing can wipe out the memory of the murderous pastrycook who served to frighten the little children of La Rue des Marmouzets.'

A second, and far more gruesome, contender as the role-model for Sweeney Todd appeared a hundred years later across the Channel in Scotland. Here, during the reign of James VI (later James I of England) a bloodthirsty young outcast named Sawney Beane started a reign of terror by preying on unsuspecting travellers in the Galloway area, first robbing and then killing his victims. What was more horrifying still was the fact that Beane then used the corpses to feed himself and his family.

There was no suggestion in the accounts about Sawney Beane that he was either a barber or turned his victims into meat pies, but there was evidence that he had been responsible for the death and cannibalism of about a thousand people during the space of twenty-five years. Not without good reason has he gone down in history as 'The Man Eater of Scotland'. (See Appendix 1)

It seemed that Sawney lived with a woman of equally profligate and vicious ways in a remote cave near the coast of Galloway from which they operated – slaughtering anyone who came into the vicinity so there would be no witnesses to their crimes. And, a contemporary report goes on, 'being destitute of any means of obtaining food, the pair resolved to live on human flesh.

'Accordingly, when they had murdered any man, woman or child, they carried them to their den, quartered them, salted and pickled the members, and dried them for food. In this manner they lived, carrying on their depredations and murders until they had eight sons and six daughters, eighteen grandsons and fourteen granddaughters, all the offspring of incest.'

As the numbers of victims of Sawney Beane and his family mounted, so did the public outcry. The horror was intensified when a number of corpses, for which the killers obviously had no need, were discovered on the Galloway seashore. Finally, word was sent to Edinburgh and the authorities mounted a campaign of action.

Months of searching throughout Galloway failed to locate Sawney Beane – though several times groups of men passed the cave without realising anyone lived there. Finally, a party with bloodhounds, one of whom 'raised up an uncommon barking and noise' at the entrance to the cave, tracked the cannibals to their 'habitation of horrid cruelty'.

The hideaway proved to be about a mile in length and contained a network of passages and tunnels. The sights which confronted the members of the party who entered the gloomy, stench-ridden interior were almost beyond description, and made many of the men physically ill – as another account testifies:

'Legs, arms, thighs, hands and feet of men, women and children were suspended in rows like dried beef. Some limbs and other members were soaked in pickle; while a great mass of money, both of gold and silver, watches, rings, pistols, cloths, both woollen and linen, with an inconceivable quantity of other articles, were either thrown together in heaps or suspended on the sides of the cave.'

Not without difficulty, the wild family were rounded up. Then, after the human remains had been buried, the party returned to Edinburgh. A day later, Sawney Beane and his tribe were executed in Leith Walk without any formal trial, 'it being deemed unnecessary to try those who were avowed enemies to all mankind and of all social order,' the account says.

According to this same report, the manner of the death of Sawney Beane and his family was appropriate to the enormity of their crimes: the men all had their testicles and penises cut off, followed by their hands and legs, after which they were allowed to bleed slowly to death; the women, in the meantime, were made to watch the death of their menfolk and were afterwards all burned together on three huge bonfires.

Such is the story of Sawney Beane; and the connection between him and Sweeney Todd was first advanced in 1901 in the pages of the magazine. *Notes & Queries,* by a writer who signed himself, 'Gnomon'.

'I have always been under the impression,' 'Gnomon' wrote, 'that the legend of the Demon Barber of Fleet Street was suggested by the incidents of a *cause célèbre* in Scotland of the sixteenth century. This was the revolting trial of Sawney Beane and his associates transferred to London and Fleet Street where, to my personal knowledge, a penny pie-shop carried on its business in the forties of the last century on the very site attributed to it in the tale. Whether the adjacent house (at that date thriving as a cook-shop, conspicuous for that succulent kind of Yorkshire pudding described by Dickens in *David Copperfield* under the name of 'spotted covey' from the raisins liberally adorning its greasy surface) was a barber's shop once I do not know.

'These two apparently very ancient houses stood about the centre of a group extending from the east corner of St Dunstan's Churchyard to the south-west corner of Fetter Lane. Many readers will remember them, for they were demolished but a very few years ago; their upper stories were of wood, and they were surmounted by a peculiar wood parapet or balustrade gallery overlooking the busy thoroughfare below. When the pie-shop discontinued purveying its special comestibles (and I have, as a boy, many times "sampled" its excellent wares), it was carried on as a bookseller's business under the conduct of a dealer of extremely peculiar views named Truelove, who also long ago disappeared.'

Of 'Gnomon's' theory, I have to say that for a man who adopted a soubriquet meaning 'Indicator', I find the connection between the two killers tenuous in the extreme! The information he provides about the shops beside St Dunstan's is, however, a little more relevant to the real story of Sweeney Todd as we shall see later.

A century later, during the reign of Charles II (1630-1685), another series of events occurred which lead to the suggestion that Sweeney Todd might have been inspired not by a man, but by a similarly evil female barber! Women barbers were apparently fairly commonplace in London in the seventeenth century – several of them being based at Seven Dials.

This particular story is related by John Thomas Smith in his *Ancient Topgraphy of London* (1810). 'On one occasion,' he writes, 'that I might indulge the humour of being shaved by a woman, I repaired to the Seven Dials where, in Great St Andrew's Street, a slender female performed the operation, while her husband, a strapping soldier in the Horse Guards, sat smoking his pipe. There was a famous woman in Swallow Street who shaved, and I recollect a black woman in Butcher Row, a street formerly standing by the side of St Clement's Church, near Temple Bar, who is said to have shaved with dexterity.

'Mr Thomas Batrich, the entertaining and venerable barber of Drury Lane, informs me that he has read of the Barberess of Drury Lane who shamefully maltreated her customers in the reign of Charles the Second. It was said that this woman robbed her victims and when brought to trial her premises were found to be full of stolen goods. Mr Batrich made the sinister suggestion that she might have been the model for that story of the Demon Barber of Fleet Street.'

Again, this is not a suggestion I think we can take too seriously, although it is fascinating to learn of the existence of lady barbers who also nursed the same criminal intentions towards their unsuspecting customers.

In 1800 a French barber, or *peruquier,* was involved in some grisly acts of murder that marked him down as another suspect of the real Sweeney Todd. The man apparently carried out his profession in a 'long and dismal ancient street', the Rue-de-la-Harpe in the Faubourg St Marcello. For years he was regarded as a hard-working and conscientious barber, until word began to spread that a number of customers seen entering his shop were never seen to leave. Suspicions grew – and were then gruesomely confirmed when two friends from the provinces happened to stop in the shop for a shave before continuing into the city to do some business. An account, translated from the French, which appeared in *The Tell Tale* magazine of 1825, informs us what happened next. (See Appendix 2).

'These incautious travellers, whilst in the shop of this fiend, unhappily talked of the money they had about them. After being shaved, one of the men left on an errand and promised to return for his friend. The wretched barber, who was a robber and murderer by profession, as soon as the one turned his back, drew his razor across the throat of the other and plundered him.

'On his return, the other traveller was not content with the barber's explanation that his friend had left to find him. Getting no satisfaction from his enquiries, the traveller informed the authorities of his suspicions and they returned to the premises. There, despite the protestations of the *pemquier,* the premises were searched from top to bottom. The evidence of his crimes was found in every room.

'The remainder of the story is almost too horrible for human ears, but is not upon that account less credible. The barber was in partnership with a pastrycook in the Rue-de-la-Harpe whose shop was so remarkable for savory patties that they were sent for from the most distant parts of Paris. Those who were murdered by the razor of the one were concealed by the knife of the other in those very identical patties by which, independently of his partnership in those frequent robberies, he had made a fortune.

'This case was of so terrific a nature, it was made part of the sentence of the law, that besides the execution of the monsters upon the rack, the houses in which they perpetrated those infernal deeds should be pulled down, and that the spot on which they stood should be marked out to posterity with horror and execration.'

Tempting as it might be to see this account as the basis for the Sweeney Todd legend – if we were to accept him as fiction – there are several important reasons why this cannot be so. Firstly, it is most convenient that the shops where the murderous deeds were committed should have been raised to the ground so that no evidence remained. Secondly, there is no documentation in French criminal records of any such trial of a *peruquier* and a pastrycook in the year 1800. And, thirdly, the account in *The Tell Tale* appeared almost a quarter of a century *after* the events in London which were to bring Sweeney Todd to the gallows. If there is an explanation for this tale, surely, it is that the anonymous author plagiarised the events from their British setting and moved the story in its entirety to Paris. Xenophobia triumphs!

Three other sources of the story have also come to my notice. There is a German legend of a murderous barber operating in Cologne during the early years of the eighteenth century which, I would suggest, falls into the same category as the Rue-de-la-Harpe story; while in *Notes & Queries,* a reader named Alban Doran wrote in October 1878:

'Ten years ago I read in a French paper an incident which was said to have occurred in Morocco in the spring of the same year. But it was a tale of our old friend, Sweeney Todd. The same legend, hardly differing from the French version, is to be found in *Les Rues de Paris* published in 1844.'

The third discovery is more intriguing – and opens up another debate that the Sweeney Todd legend could be rooted in an even earlier account of a cannibalistic barber operating in Calais in the *Seventeenth* Century. The story is told by a Swedish mariner, Peter

Martensson Lindstrom, who stopped in the French port en route to America in 1654 and there heard tales of a barber and a pie-maker who worked in conjunction to murder victims and turn the bodies into pies. Lindstrom was a cartographer and engineer who set sail on board the *Eagle* for the colony of New Sweden on the Delaware where he planned to make a new life. He was clearly an educated and literate man who kept a diary of his voyage and subsequent life in America. This document remained unknown until 1925 when it was translated and published by the Swedish Colonial Society of America.

Lindstrom's voyage included a stop at Dover before the *Eagle* docked in Calais where he found, according to his manuscript, 'many delicious, palatable and rare pies being baked.' These, he says, 'were the produce of a barber and pie-baker in company and council together – the former sold the human flesh to the latter with which he baked the above mentioned pies.' A pair of travelling students had apparently lead to the discovery of the terrible crimes, Lindstrom explains, when one went missing after a visit to the barber's shop. His suspicious friend thereupon called in a law officer who 'stepped on a trap door in the barber's shop and fell down into the cellar which was as full of skulls and skeletons as a charnel house in a churchyard.' (See Appendix 3).

But what of the various accounts of Sweeny Todd's life in *fictional* form? They all have something to offer about his origins and claim a basis in *fact:* albeit their versions differ from one to the next. Two typical examples will demonstrate my point. The first is from the pages of *Sweeney Todd, The Demon Barber of Fleet Street* published by Charles Fox in 1878 and claims to be a direct quote from the lips of the serial killer himself following his arrest:

'I do not know my own birth-date. The church I was christened in was burnt down only the day after and all the record books burned. My father and mother are dead, the nurse who brought me into the world was hanged and the doctor cut his own throat.'

By contrast the details in *The Life of Sweeney Todd, Demon Barber of Fleet Street,* published in 1912 by the Daisy Bank Printing and Publishing Company in Wellington Street, Gorton, Manchester, are almost prosaic. They must be read, though, in the knowledge that this was a firm who specialised in highly romanticised tales of crime and had already published lurid versions of the lives of the Body Snatchers, Burke and Hare, Palmer the Poisoner and *The Crippen Horror:*

'From the information that has been collected, Sweeney Todd was a native of the north of England. He came to London and was in very great poverty when he opened a small barber's shop in Crutched Friars. He remained in that shop about seventeen months and then paid £125 pounds for the lease of a house in Fleet Street. For this he was only to pay a rental to the Skinners Company of £17.10s per annum, having agreed to keep the premises in good repair. The lower part of the house had been a small hosier's, but he altered it into a barber's shop and there resided until his arrest on the serious charges that will now be related.'

The more this kind of conflicting evidence is examined, the clearer it became to me that Sweeney Todd had not been modelled on anyone else. He was an original from whom others had seen fit to borrow. Indeed, the true story of the man who would become known as 'The Demon Barber of Fleet Street' is like so much fact – far stranger than fiction; and, equally, more interesting and gruesome than any of these alleged prototypes, as the following pages will reveal.

The Road To Crime

Sweeney Todd was born on 26 October, 1756, in Brick Lane, Stepney. The actual house in which the child first breathed the fetid air of a London slum is not known, though it has been suggested it may have been one of a trio of three-storey buildings, numbers 85, 87 or 89, on the west side of the street, near the junction with Hanbury Street and just a stone's throw from Spitalfields Market.

According to the Royal Commission on Historical Monuments, carried out in 1930, the three tall properties, with their distinctive brick bands between the upper stories, had been in existence since the early eighteenth century, though by the middle of the century they were already showing signs of decay through overcrowding and neglect. It was in the attic of one of these that Sweeney Todd's mother, not yet twenty, gave birth to her son. She scratched a meagre living in winding silk. Her husband was a silk weaver.

The birth was not an easy one by all accounts, and Mrs Todd would have no more children. Her husband, because of the uncertain nature of his profession, had, like many of his fellows, already taken to heavy drinking and would consequently play little part in the rearing of his son. ('Gin', says historian David Hughson in his *History of London* [1806], 'was said to be the drink of the more sedentary trades, weavers particularly, and of women' – it was essentially a disease of poverty, so cheap, so warming and brought such forgetfulness of cold and misery.')

The omens for both the child and his parents were far from promising, although Sweeney Todd was to claim later, 'My mother used to make quite a pet of me. I was fondled and kissed and called a pretty boy. But later I used to wish I was strong enough to throttle her. What the devil did she bring me into the world for unless she had plenty of money to give me so that I might enjoy myself in it?'

London in the last quarter of the eighteenth century was indeed a city of enormous contrasts. On the one hand there were the rich houses, magnificent churches, fine theatres and prosperous mercantile buildings, and almost literally back-to-back with them the appalling, disease-ridden slums and dens of vice and depravity that almost defied description. Indeed the face of London was that of a prosperous, developing metropolis, but behind the facade lurked another world of desperation and poverty where men and women struggled for an existence. The life of the well-to-do was something this luckless mass of humanity in their sordid underworld could only look on with envy, and drown their frustration in a tide of ale, gin and debauchery.

It is a period of history that, although well-served by documents and records, has been perhaps best captured in illustration by one of the most brilliant of all British painters and engravers, William Hogarth (1697-1764). Although his superb series of drawings like *Industry and Idleness, Gin Lane, Beer Street* and *The Four Stages of Cruelty* were all completed by the middle of the century, little had changed twenty years on and they still represented the lot of 'men and women of the lowest ranks'. In them is to be seen the brutality and depravity of London life and the seeming hopelessness in which a large portion of the nation found itself. Life, to be sure, was cheap, crime and murder were commonplace, and deportation or the rope seemed scarcely worse alternatives than the situation the poor citizen already found himself in.

The last decades of the century were uncertain times, too, not helped by the cruel label of 'mad' which was attached to the monarch, George III (1738-1820) and the open corruption and self-serving of so many of those m his court, parliament and official circles. George, indeed, had been almost swept under by adverse circumstances since his accession, and even though he made resolute efforts to uphold the honour of England and the crown, his own limitations and the inexorable course of world events were against him.

In hindsight, the reign of George III was an extraordinary one, spanning sixty years from 1760 to 1820: the longest of any British King. (Only his granddaughter, Queen Victoria, has sat longer on the throne.) His was a reign, also, which saw two crucial events in world history, the breakaway from Britain of the American colonies and later the French Revolution, both of which had major effects on the nation and her international role. Although at the time of both occurrences,

George was by no stretch of the imagination insane, he had already suffered bouts of madness and to much of the world – including many of his own people – he was already 'The Mad King'.

George III was the eldest son of Frederick, Prince of Wales. 'Poor Fred' as he was known, was a weak, insecure man who died in 1751, leaving his thirteen-year-old son his title and much of his character. But George had a strong-minded, domineering mother, Augusta, who, as she sensed the reign of his grandfather, George II, growing towards its end, began to exert her will so that in the fullness of time she might be the real power behind her son's throne. When, in 1760, the old king died suddenly and George III was proclaimed, Augusta had him firmly under her control. At twenty-two and having lived a most sheltered existence, he was no match for his mother's wiles, nor indeed for those others in power who sought to shape his opinions and decisions. In a sentence, he showed himself too trusting and naive of all those he came in contact with.

Under such circumstances, it comes as no surprise to find corruption growing rife and unscrupulous power-seeking everywhere, and even the hope that George might find a strong-willed wife, who would provide him with less biased guidance, was thwarted by Augusta. She selected for him a quiet and inoffensive German Princess, Charlotte, who became Queen in 1761.

There is no doubt that George tried hard to master the complexities of kingship and state, and much of his later illness can doubtless be seen to have been increased by the pressures exerted on him by his mother, his own family problems, and the unsettled times at home and abroad. The first major crisis, of course, came in the 1770's with the troubles which erupted in the American colony under British rule. At first George was persuaded by his advisers that this was merely the work of a few trouble makers, and was quite blinded to the seriousness of the situation. He, along with his subjects, was outraged over the famous incident which has gone down in history as the 'Boston Tea Party' and which, in the fullness of time, led to the full-scale War of Independence. It is to George's eternal credit that he had no desire to inflict war on his subjects in the Americas, and against the advice of some of his ministers was prepared to sue for peace with the colonists for any price short of independence. This, of course, was not acceptable to the Americans and with the Declaration of Independence on July 4 1776, the final nail was driven into the coffin of Britain's hopes of retaining its hold over the colony.

It was George himself who suffered most deeply over the loss of America, for the people attributed it directly to his unbalanced handling of the situation. Nor was his peace of mind helped any by his eldest son, George, the Prince of Wales, who was taking full advantage of his father's preoccupation and general laxity to lead a life of debauchery. In vain the king sought to reason with his son, and at the same time save his own declining health. But it was yet another battle he was doomed to lose: for not long after he suffered his first attack of madness, and although he had periodic bouts of good health thereafter, he was never fully fit again for any length of time.

However, it is only true to say that the King was completely insane during the last ten years of his life. Prior to this – although on occasions his mind wandered and he could change from moods of gentleness to towering rage – he was firmly enough in charge of his faculties to govern the country to the best of his limited abilities and as well as those around him would allow him.

With the benefit of hindsight and increased medical knowledge, we now know that what George was actually suffering from was a rare disease known as porphyria, a disturbance of the porphyrin metabolism, and a complaint not fully understood until this century. This is the process producing the pigments which give blood its red colour, and if there is more of the pigment in the body than is needed by the blood, the urine becomes discoloured and the whole nervous system, including the brain, is poisoned. Porphyria can exist in varying degrees of severity; delirium only occurs in extreme cases and it is possible for the sufferer to have attacks which vary in intensity. According to doctors, Porphyria can be transmitted from generation to generation, and medical experts who have studied George's case history believe that the diagnosis is further supported by milder symptoms of the same disease appearing in other members of his family, including his sister, four of his sons, and several of his German relatives.

Such, then, was the condition of the man who ruled Britain during the later part of the Eighteenth Century. It was this weakness of body and mind that those closest to him exploited to inflict their own mean ambitions on the population.

This population was rapidly increasing and consequently with more able-bodied men available than jobs to fill, unscrupulous factory operators and land owners could keep down wages to suit themselves. The labourer was thus in no position to bargain for a better deal, and so he found himself beset on both sides – with poor wages on which to try and keep himself and his family, and on the other side a corrupt administration to which he had no hope of turning for redress. Life was hard, and there was a sense of despair that pervaded the minds of many citizens like the Todd family in Stepney.

Certainly, the world into which Sweeney was born has rightly been described as, 'the beginning of a Dark Age in which there was a progressive degredation of the standards of life under the blight of growing industrialisation', by the historian Dorothy George in her definitive study, *London Life in the Eighteenth Century* (1930).

Mrs George adds: 'Throughout the century, Londoners lived in a world where violence, disorder and brutal punishment were still part of the normal background of life. Newgate, the gallows, the exploits of felons, figured largely in the press and in the current literature of the day. In spite of the bitter irony of Jonathan Wild and the light satire of the *Beggars' Opera,* both are accurate pictures of the manners of the time, and their more lurid incidents are easily surpassed in the records of the Old Bailey.'

The London of 1756 was certainly unrecognisable from today. The population of the city numbered 670,000, which would rise to over 900,000 by the end of the century. Unlike today, it also consisted of a number of self-contained communities: partly due to the difficulty of getting from one part of the town to the other; partly due to the rigid lines between classes, trades and occupations; and mostly because of the dangerous character of many districts which did not encourage casual visitors. The Spitalfields area where Sweeney Todd was born was just such a district – much of it a slum shielding every kind of squalor and savagery, and home to many criminal dens. In the year 1750, according to the *Commons Journals,* it consisted of 2,400 houses, 1000 of which were not rated 'being inhabited by journeymen weavers and other artificers and labourers who cannot support themselves and their families without credit for small sums'.

The Todds as a family were forever in debt, and always on the verge of the starvation and misery which beset the weaving industry during the second half of the eighteenth century. Spitalfields was then known as the silk-weaving district of London, the leading manufacturers living in places such as Spital Square while their weavers occupied any tenement or garret they could find nearby. These men were chiefly employed in making ribbons – which were then very much in fashion – or broad silks for the gentry. Most of the weavers worked in small factories, although a few – the more highly skilled – owned or hired their own looms and sold on the silks they produced to the manufacturers. The recurring problem for both master and man was always the same, though – getting paid, as a report of 1764 reveals:

'Many London manufacturers and especially weavers are sometimes much streightened for money, either to pay their men's wages or to find goods to employ them, especially at the dead time of year, and therefore, being forced to pawn some of their goods for what pawnbrokers are pleased to lend on them, they do not only impoverish themselves, and turn away their men, who, for want of work, do with their families become a burthen to the public. Many manufacturers have of late discharged fifty to a hundred men and put as many more upon half work; and in a little time after the distress has been beyond description . . .'

A specific report on the industry in Spitalfields at this same period goes even further: 'The poverty and distress of some of these people is inconceivable; very generally a family in every room with very little bedding, furniture or clothes. The few rags on their backs comprise the principal part of their property.'

Sweeney Todd's father had experienced years of this kind of uncertain living and, as one of the less skilled weavers, rarely earned more than 12 to 15 shillings per week. Even this sum was often under threat from emigrant Irish workers who would accept less, or women and children who could be employed for even smaller amounts. (A woman like Mrs Todd would probably be hired to wind silk at no more than 3 shillings per week.) Occasionally, Mr Todd would be forced to accept the most menial work of all: winding silk onto bobbins which had to be done at home. Evidence suggests he forced his wife and his infant son into doing this task for him, beating them whenever he became drunk.

Apart from the harshness at home, one of young Sweeney's earliest memories was of the famous Spitalfields Silk Weavers Riots which took place in 1765 when he was just ten years old. The mounting sense of unrest among the local weavers about the growing importation of cheap calico which was undercutting their wages finally exploded into violence. The weavers attacked women and girls on the streets who were wearing calico, throwing acid onto their clothes or tearing the gowns off their backs. Soldiers had to be called in to quell the rioters and, during the ensuing melee, five weavers were shot and killed.

The violence both frightened and excited young Sweeney Todd. He vowed there and then that his father's profession was not for him – there had to be a better and easier way of making money.

The boy had, though, already found one place to escape from the drudgery of his daily life – the Tower of London which was less than a mile away from his home. It was an ideal place to go when his parents were either drunkenly brawling or asleep.

There was something about the grim and sombre mass of the Tower and its association with the darker history of England ever since it had been built by William the Conqueror in 1078, that appealed to young Sweeney's increasingly gloomy nature. He had, after all, little to smile about in his life and took a ghoulish sense of pleasure from haunting the edifice on the banks of the River Thames. The awe which the huge building was intended to inspire in the citizens of London certainly had its influence upon him.

Today, of course, the Tower serves primarily as a museum; but in its time it has also been a fortress, royal palace, armoury, mint, and, perhaps most surprisingly of all, until 1835 it was also a royal zoo. It was, though, primarily intended as a prison for political prisoners. Within its massive and forbidding walls, many distinguished men and women were incarcerated including four kings and such famous historical figures as Sir Thomas More, Anne Boleyn, Lady Jane Grey and Archbishop Laud. For many, their stay in the Tower of London ended with a short walk to the scaffold.

The fortress was not only famous for its prisoners, but also its unique collection of instruments of torture which the public was allowed to view in the hope it would discourage them from crime or civil disobedience. Young Todd, we are told, came first to peer at the animals in the zoo and then to linger over the bloodied torture weapons.

The Lion Tower was a favourite spot with many visitors. It housed a number of superb lions as well as several tigers, leopards, black bears and wolves. The warders, however, had none of the finer feelings of the modern zoo attendants – they apparently delighted in poking the creatures with long poles 'to make them lively for visitors,' according to a mid-eighteenth century account. This same source relates that one incautious warden who stuck his arm into the lion's den had a hand bitten off, while a leopard that broke loose 'jumped on the back of a sentinal and half ate him up'.

Excited by watching the lions being fed on huge beef bones of a kind that had never once crossed the Todd's table, Sweeney would then visit the places of torture and feast his eyes on the instruments of madness and death. There was the 'Little Ease', a hole under the White Tower just 18 inches wide, 4 feet high and 2 feet deep into which a prisoner would be forced so that his head was pressed down onto his chest and he could neither sit down or lean. Perhaps even more ghastly were the lower cells which flooded when the tide came in and were also plagued with starving rats. Here prisoners were put for the purpose of extorting confessions: as the water rose, the unfortunate occupants risked death either by drowning or by having the flesh torn from their backs by the sharp teeth of the ravening hoardes of rodents.

In the rooms through which Sweeney Todd roamed were to be seen terrifying thumbscrews; the 'iron gauntlets' which suspended a prisoner from the ceiling by his hands; the fearsome rack that could literally tear a prisoner's joints from his sockets; and the notorious 'Scavenger's Daughter'. This consisted of iron hoops which were tightened around a victim's body by the executioner until blood began to spurt from every orifice and death seemed like a mercy.

Today such sights would probably be considered unsuitable viewing for impressionable young minds, but dozens of urchins from the slums like Sweeney Todd feasted their eyes on these horrors and listened with rapt attention whenever a warden proceeded to give a suitably embellished and invariably gruesome description of their use to visitors.

There was, however, nothing to attract Sweeney – or anyone else for that matter – to the nearby River Thames in the 1760s. An odious mixture of household refuse, plus the waste from factories and open latrines along the banks – all of which poured directly into the Thames – had earned it the reputation of the dirtiest river in Europe. Small wonder that those who ventured near the water, which varied in colour from dark green to black, ran a very real danger of contracting cholera, typhus, smallpox or tuberculosis.

Only during the depth of winter did the Thames hold any sort of attraction for Londoners. For during particularly hard winters, the river froze over and 'Frost Fairs' would be held on the ice when rows of booths would be set up offering food, drink and amusements. Records indicate that there were a number of famous 'Frost Fairs' during the eighteenth century, including one in 1715 – of which there are numerous illustrations – and another in 1739 when frost and strong winds also combined to cause £100,000 damage to shipping in the river and froze a number of people to death on land and at sea.

A more prolonged winter still hit London in 1768 when Sweeney Todd was twelve years old. Although the Thames froze over, few people had any thought of enjoying themselves, so intense was the cold. As one bitterly cold week followed another, coal became increasingly scarce and expensive and few people had the means of maintaining any kind of continual heating. Dozens died in their own homes, and a shoemaker found frozen to death in his stall was just one of several tradespeople who went to work when he should have remained at home.

Among those who did remain at home were the Todd family in Brick Lane. With no work, Sweeney's parents spent their last money on gin and ignored the plaintive cries of their desperate son. Their agony did not continue long, however. For Sweeney awoke one morning as the pale grey light of another bitterly cold day broke into the tenement to find that both his parents had gone. He was never to see either again. Not surprisingly, he nursed a resentment against both for the rest of his life.

Quite what happened to the Todds is unknown: possibly they went searching for more gin and died of cold in the streets. If so, their bodies would have been heaped up with all the others who collapsed in the streets during that terrible winter, and then thrown into a pauper's grave. Certainly, Sweeney Todd never found out what had happened to his parents, although later when arrested for his crimes he invented another typically outrageous lie about his origins and parenthood.

'The church I was christened at was burnt down the day after, and all the books burned,' he told one of his interrogators. 'My father and mother are dead, and the nurse was hanged and the doctor cut his throat.'

There is mystery, too, surrounding the details of how Sweeney himself survived that terrible winter and was next heard of working as an apprentice to a cutler in Holborn. It is reasonable to conject that the resourcefulness and cunning which were later to serve him so well when he began his career of crime came to his aid then, too.

Child labour was a part of every London trade and each tradesman had his apprentice – some even had several. Those children whose parents had been able to give them a basic education could be apprenticed to a tradesman on payment of a fee and might well expect to earn a few pounds a year during their apprenticeship. But what of the others like Sweeney Todd? Historian Dorothy George explains the fate of all such orphans of the streets:

'One of the worst results of the social conditions of this period was the large number of children entirely abandoned to the streets as vagrants or thrown on the tender mercies of the parish. It was the duty of the parish according to the famous Act of 1601 to nurse all of these and to apprentice them when they were old enough.

'Any person, master or journeyman, man or woman, housekeeper or lodger, who would undertake to provide food, lodging and instruction, could take an apprentice. All the earnings of that apprentice, whether they were for the master or a third person, became the property of the master.'

Such a system was obviously open to the most terrible abuses, and Mrs George quotes a report of 1768 which graphically highlights the plight of many youngsters:

'The master may be a tiger in cruelty, he may beat, abuse, strip naked, starve or do what he will to the poor innocent lad, few people take much notice, and the officers who put him out the least of anybody. The greatest part of those who now take poor apprentices are the most indigent and dishonest, and it is the fate of many a poor child, not only to be half-starved and sometimes bred up in no trade, but to be forced to thieve and steal for his master, and so is brought to the gallows into the bargain.'

There is no evidence that Sweeney Todd's master was any better or worse than these men, but he certainly played a part in setting the boy on the road to the gallows.

John Crook was the singularly appropriate name of the man to whom Sweeney Todd was bound. His shop was in Great Turnstile, Holborn. The sign above his window combined a pistol and the letter 'C' which stood for his name.

Cutlers in the eighteenth century were, in fact, dexterous and ingenious artisans who made a whole variety of objects including 'Tinder boxes, Toothpick Cases, Gun Hammers, Wig Springs, Back-Gammon Tables, Saw Strops, Squirrel Chains, Tobacco Tongs, Line Rowls and "Best Battle Gunpowder"' according to the advertisement of one such London tradesman.

It appears that John Crook was also something of a specialist in razors, for his name is to be found listed with half a dozen other razor makers in London at this time including Edward Tymperon who had premises in Drury Lane and a certain Alexander Jolly to be found at the sign of 'The Unicorn & Case of Knives' in Compton Street, Soho.

Though nothing is actually known about Sweeney Todd's apprenticeship with John Crook, it certainly lasted for at least two years. That he learned a good deal from his master is also fairly evident because of the skill he was later to show in designing and operating the revolving chair in his barber shop. It also seems quite safe to assume that he learned all about razors.

The relationship between the apprentice and his master came to an abrupt end sometime during the year of 1770, however. The boy was accused of petty theft, hauled before a magistrate, and sentenced to five years imprisonment in Newgate Prison. He was just fourteen years old.

Harsh as this sentence seems today, Sweeney Todd was, in fact, quite lucky to escape with his life. For at this time there were still more than 200 crimes on the statute books that were punishable by hanging – and these included such simple acts as stealing more than a shilling as a pick-pocket or taking goods worth more than 25 pence from a shop.

Whatever Sweeney Todd's crime was, there seems little doubt that he entered prison feeling even more bitter at life. And there that bitterness was to turn first to resentment, and then to a burning desire for revenge.

The Cut-Throat Killer

Newgate Prison, into which the young Sweeney Todd was unceremoniously bundled in 1770, was a massive and grim fortress which stood on the site occupied today by the Central Criminal Court, the Old Bailey. Indeed, it is an interesting fact that when the notorious gaol was finally pulled down in 1904 some of its stones were used in the building of the present famous London courthouse.

Newgate was, in 1770, one of seven London gates which marked the boundaries of the city: the others were Ludgate, Moorgate, Cripplegate, Bishopsgate, Aldersgate and Aldgate. Temple Bar, which also features in our story, was also a gate erected for ceremonial purposes at the extent of the city liberties.

In company with the city's other western gates – Ludgate and Cripplegate – Newgate served as a prison, though in its case it was primarily for the custody of the common criminals of London and Middlesex. The great grey edifice spanned the roadway of Newgate Street and consisted of two annexes, four storeys high, which were linked by staircases and passageways. The exterior of the building was ornamented with pilasters and statues, one of these being the figure of Liberty with a cat coiled at her feet – and therein lay a story.

From the twelfth century, only the chambers on top of Newgate had served as a gaol, but it had become a prison proper in the fifteenth century thanks to money donated in the will of Sir Richard Whittington – the legendary mayor who walked to London with his cat – who had died in 1423. However, the building suffered badly in the Great Fire of London in 1666 and was almost completely rebuilt. By the late eighteenth century it had become notorious throughout the kingdom.

Apart from the dank and stiffling cells of Newgate which had earned it a terrifying reputation among the law-breaking fraternity, the prison was also notorious with the general public because of the distinguished list of its inmates. This included such master criminals as the pirate, Captain Kidd; James McLean the highwayman; the 'prince of thieves' Jonathan Wild; and the great escaper, Jack Sheppard. Alongside these luminaries were any number of pick-pockets, forgers, burglars and petty thieves of all descriptions. Their ages ranged from mere children of ten to old lags in their seventies. One famous visitor to Newgate, Charles Dickens, was so struck by the young pick-pockets he saw there that he used a group of them as the models for his famous novel, *Oliver Twist,* first published in serial form between 1837 and 1839.

A favourite pastime of certain Londoners was to come and stare at the criminals in Newgate – especially the notorious ones like James McLean and Jack Sheppard. On payment of about three shillings, these visitors were allowed to enter the forbidding walls and stare at the unfortunates in their cells. The more fashionable visitor always made sure they carried a handkerchief soaked in vinegar to counteract the fetid air of the prison and its inmates.

Prior to 1728 many common criminals like Sweeney Todd had been thrown into the Condemned Hold, a mass dungeon on the ground floor that had only a solitary window and was entered by a heavy door topped with spikes which opened onto the entrance hallway of the prison. This had now been replaced by fifteen new cells. Each measured just 9 feet by 7 feet, and was illuminated by a double-grated window. Here the prisoners lived out much of their sentences, although they were allowed out to visit the 'day room' where they could mingle with friends and – if they had any money – receive visitors.

For many years, the gaolers at Newgate had supplemented their meagre wages by extorting money from prisoners. In the main this would 'buy' the men visits from family and relatives, though the more unscrupulous custodians would also threaten to place those who had committed petty crimes in the same cells as violent criminals unless they were paid off. Though this practice was by no means as prevalent when young Todd entered Newgate, those prisoners who had the wherewithal to grease a gaoler's palm certainly enjoyed an easier time of it during their sentence.

Money was, in fact, necessary to even survive in Newgate – for without it a prisoner would soon find himself short of proper clothing to protect himself from the dankness and cold, or without a reg supply of food that was edible. Quickly realising this, the young Sweeney Todd lost no time in looking for an opportunity to keep himself warm and fed. He found it in the shape of a grizzled old barber named Plummer who was serving ten years for embezzlement.

Plummer had apparently swindled money from one of his fashionable London clients, and was then in the fourth year of his imprisonment. He had not wasted the years, though – for there were plenty of the better-off prisoners who liked a shave, and anyone who fell ill had no one but the barber to turn to for treatment.

At this period of time in history, the barber actually played a considerably more extensive role in society than today: he was, in fact, both hairdresser and doctor. People went to him for shaves and haircuts as well as treatment for any minor bodily complaints. Some barbers were even surgeons and quite capable of performing minor operations such as removing a gangrenous arm or leg. Indeed, the ability to wield a blade on human flesh and bones was a prequisite of real success in the trade. (Records indicate that some London barbers even traded in spirits – a useful sideline, no doubt, with customers about to go under the knife who would doubtless be more than willing to pay for a strong tot or two of brandy!)

It is interesting to note that the famous striped pole which has been a feature outside barbers' shops for many years is a remnant from these days. The pole itself represents the staff which the 'barber-surgeon' gave his patient to hold while he was being bled, to encourage the blood to flow. The red, black or blue band painted around the pole represents the ribbon or garter with which the arm of the customer was bound up after the operation.

In a filthy and disease-ridden place like Newgate, the services of the barber Plummer were no doubt much in demand. And Sweeney Todd had the good fortune to enter the prison just as the youngster who had served as the barber's assistant – or 'soap boy' – was being discharged. The new inmate lost no time in boasting to Plummer that he had worked for a cutler and was experienced in sharpening razors and generally looking after the implements of a barber's trade. Whether he told the older man precisely *why* he was now incarcerated we have no way of knowing.

Plummer was evidently impressed enough by the boy to give him the job. He may also have liked Sweeney's touch of cunning, for the barber was still up to his old tricks swindling money from fellow prisoners and gaolers alike. There is no doubt Sweeney Todd learned quickly from his new master – becoming dextrous with the soap brush and deft at lifting small change from the pockets of his master's clients as they reclined in his chair. The boy had, of course, to hand over these ill-gotten gains to Plummer, but was happy to do so in return for the food and clothing and occasional privileges the job earned him. He was, though, always sorry to see the barber's razors carefully collected up by the gaolers at the end of each day – for he would dearly have loved to purloin one for his own use. It seemed obvious to the boy that it was as easy to scrape the whiskers from a man's chin as it would be to slit his throat while he sat, so unaware and vulnerable, in the shaving chair. Clearly, Fate was inexhorably moving Sweeney Todd closer towards his destiny.

Those prisoners about to be executed were always allowed a special shave before they were hung and Todd invariably accompanied Plummer on these assignments. It was the one place that conversation was permitted, too; for in the main part of Newgate a rule of silence was rigidly enforced and those who broke it were flogged. And as the condemned man had probably recently received visitors, it was another way of finding out what was happening in the world beyond the walls of Newgate.

The public outside were evidently just as interested in what was going on *inside* Newgate, for a year after Sweeney Todd had entered the prison, the first issue of a weekly, penny publication, *The Newgate Calendar; or, Malefactor's Bloody Register,* was issued by an astute London publisher named J. Cooke. This famous record of crimes and trials was undoubtedly a forerunner of the most sensational of today's tabloid newspapers. Its aim – according to a banner on the front page – was to feature 'Genuine and Circumstantial Narratives of the Lives and Transactions, Various Exploits and Dying Speeches, of the Most Notorious Criminals of Both Sexes.'

The publication, printed in double columns of miniscule type on eight pages of flimsy paper, featured a single lurid illustration on the front cover, and inside all the most gruesome and dramatic tales of forgery, robbery and murder the editor could unearth. The earliest cases were from 1700 and virtually every one ended in a hanging.

The success of *The Newgate Calendar* was to inspire several imitators, as well as generating an interest in true crime that has continued to flourish and develop to the present day. As historian Rayner Heppenstall wrote in his *Reflections on the Newgate Calendar* (1975):

'The *Newgate Calendar* itself is literature, for the most part of a rather poor kind, fit only to inspire literature in others. The best of it is evidence heard in court, which, once transcribed and published, is literature. Law itself is literature. In court, lawyers compose literature with great deliberation. The spontaneous cut-and-thrust of courtroom drama on stage, screen or radio is rarely heard in court. There, judges and counsel dictate their works slowly to the clerk of the court and to reporters, much as Henry James dictated his to a devoted secretary or as modern authors may dictate theirs to tape recorders, with all the more care because it will not be possible for them to make alterations in the transcript.'

Mr Heppenstall also adds, 'The later Calendars were among the first products of a reforming age which looked back fascinated at one during which too many were hanged for too little.'

The Newgate Calendar was to run in one form or another until 1825, in all covering over a thousand cases from the years 1701 to 1825. An enterprising publisher named E. Harrison who operated in Salisbury Square, Fleet Street, revived the idea in 1864 as *The New Newgate Calendar,* expanding the format to sixteen pages, but mingling fiction amongst the factual accounts of crimes, many of which had been lifted, almost untouched, from the pages of its predecessor.

A third London publisher, W. Barnes, operating from 44, Bridge-house Place, Newington Causeway, also jumped on the 'crim-con literature' bandwagon by issuing *The Annals of Crime, and New Newgate Calendar,* which sold for one penny and carried particularly gruesome illustrations above the purple prose on the front page of each issue. Barnes, like Harrison, stole his material unashamedly, revising and rewriting cases to satisfy the public demand for ever more salacious details. With this fact in mind, I have referred to all quotes hereafter from these sources under the generic title of *The Newgate Calendar.*

It is doubtful whether Sweeney Todd knew anything about *The Newgate Calendar* when it was launched – or would even have tried to read it if he did, for there is evidence that he was no more than semi-literate at the time of his arrest. He was, though, to feature in its pages when justice finally caught up with him, as we shall discover later.

Despite his association with the barber Plummer, Todd did not escape the vindictiveness of some of the Newgate gaolers or the cruelty of a number of his fellow inmates. His privileged position caused resentment among some of the other youthful offenders and he took several cruel beatings during his five year imprisonment. One convicted murderer apparently beat him to within an inch of his life when he caught the boy pilfering through his few possessions. Plummer is said to have stood by while this punishment was meted out – probably from a mixture of fear and cowardice – though he would undoubtedly have benefited from any of his soap boy's plunder.

The resentment that Sweeney Todd nursed against society certainly built up as the five years of his prison sentence dragged by; although he did not allow this to deter him from learning all about his master's profession. He already knew it would be the trade he would follow once he was released from Newgate . . .

The Sweeney Todd who at last walked free from Newgate Prison in the autumn of 1775 was now a strapping nineteen-year-old with a profession. But the years had also made him a morose, bitter and cruel man. Although it is doubtful whether he actually planned a life of crime – he had, after all, just sacrificed five years because of it – his ambition was to make money, and he had few scruples about how he was going to do this.

Sweeney's immediate need, though, was to earn his daily bread and in order to do this he joined the ranks of London's 'Flying Barbers'. These men, who were commonplace in eighteenth-century England, travelled wherever there was the likelihood of custom, setting themselves up on street corners, in markets or at fairs, and offering their services to passersby. It was a tough business where men would fight over a favourite pitch, and Sweeney Todd undoubtedly had to bloody more than a few other 'Flying Barbers' in order to survive and make his way.

But survive he did. Five years after his release from Newgate Prison, the young barber had apparently earned enough to be operating from his own premises near Hyde Park Corner. There he prospered, until one night just before Christmas 1784.

There is evidence that Todd was being helped in his business by a young woman, though what their relationship was remains a mystery. Certainly, there is no record of the barber ever marrying, though it is possible that he may have referred to her as his wife for the benefit of his more refined clientele. What we *do* know is that Sweeney Todd's temper was already getting the better of him when he became annoyed, and this unfortunate woman probably bore the brunt of his rages whenever they occurred.

The events which were to dramatically change the course of Sweeney Todd's life and lead him to the London street with which his name is now associated, occurred on 1 December 1784. They are related in a single paragraph which appeared in *The Annual Register* under the heading, 'A Barbarous Barber':

'A most remarkable murder was perpetrated in the following manner by a journeyman barber that lived near Hyde Park Corner, who had been jealous of his wife, but could in no way bring this home to her. A young gentleman, by chance coming into the barber's shop to be shaved and dressed, and being in liquor, mentioned having seen a fine girl in Hamilton Street, from whom he had had certain favours the night before, and at the same time describing her person. The barber, concluding this to be his wife, and in the height of his frenzy, cut the young gentleman's throat from ear to ear and absconded.'

The details are certainly sparse, and though the disappearing barber is not mentioned by name – as few criminals were in the press of the time until brought to trial – the events matched the known facts about Sweeney Todd's whereabouts in the last days of 1784.

Although a hue and cry was raised shortly after the discovery of the murder by the next customer who entered the barber's shop and found the blood-soaked corpse slumped in the shaving chair, no sign of the man who had shaved him was ever reported again in Hyde Park Corner. 'Mrs Todd' appears to have been none too disturbed by the disappearance, however, and rumour has it that by the New Year she was already living with another tradesman in the district.

It has to be admitted that the evidence Sweeney Todd committed this crime remains circumstantial at best. Indeed, the grounds are primarily a confession by the man himself after he was finally arrested for his serial killings.

'My first 'un was a young gent at Hyde Park Corner,' he is reported as saying. 'Slit him from ear to ear, I did.'

There is, however, no disputing the facts about where he next came to light and set up in business – Fleet Street. Nor that in the cramped and dingy front room of a little shop there, he would combine the ingenuity of a cutler with the skill of a barber to begin an era of murder and bloodshed that is unique in the annals of crime.

The Curious World of Fleet Street

No one knows why Sweeney Todd decided to set up his barber's pole outside a little shop at the higher end of Fleet Street, right in the shadow of Temple Bar, in the year 1785.

At first sight it seemed a curious choice for a man who had spent five years of his life imprisoned in another of London's city gates. But prices were undoubtedly cheaper there than in Covent Garden or Drury Lane – two of the most popular localities for the city's barbers – and it is quite feasible that the astute Todd realised his chances of success were better with fewer rivals on his doorstep. Or perhaps – just perhaps – he was already hatching his nefarious plans and wanted to distance himself from the centre of his profession. Maybe he even had some knowledge of the labyrinth of passageways beneath the street which would prove to be of great value in sustaining his terrible reign of crime for over a decade. All we can do from this distance in time is to conject . . .

The Fleet Street of the last quarter of the eighteenth century was, of course, very different from that of today. Just a few years ago it was known around the world as the 'Street of Ink', the home for some of the most important and influential newspapers in Europe including the *Daily Express,* the *Daily Telegraph,* the *Observer,* the *Daily Mail,* the *Sun* and the *News of the World.* But industrial disputes and the arrival of computer technology has seen them all depart and now only the memory remains. Fleet Street is, though, still a place worth visiting, if only to try and imagine just what it must have been like when Sweeney Todd lived there. Where today there are only orderly office buildings and commercial premises, there was then a huddle of squalid and disreputable shops, taverns and mean dwellings of all shapes and sizes. Yet the history of the place proves to be as fascinating and bizarre as any to be found within the confines of the metropolis.

Fleet Street is often wrongly associated in people's mind with the old Fleet Prison which actually stood some distance away on the eastern side of what is now Farringdon Street. It did, though, get its name from the infamous Fleet Ditch which nowadays runs in a sewer beneath Bridge Street, and was crossed by the Fleet Bridge (a site now occupied by Ludgate Circus).

For centuries the Ditch was used by the local residents as a dumping place for all their household rubbish and offal; and not surprisingly it earned an unenviable reputation for its stomach-turning appearance and appalling stench. Indeed, records indicate that the Ditch retained its filthy and insanitary state well into the eighteenth century.

The street itself had been in existence since the days of the Roman occupation of Britain, when it was a road running through open countryside crossing what was then a pleasant little stream. The walls of the Roman city of Augusta – as London was then called – ended where Ludgate Circus now stands, and a Pratorian camp was permanently located in the district. The Romans also selected the area as a burial spot for soldiers and over the years human remains of one sort and another have been found during the course of building work and excavations in Fleet Street.

Perhaps the importance that the Romans placed on the area lead to its gradual development into a fashionable district, for certainly by 1325 it was notable enough to be referred to in one history as 'Fletestrete in the suburb of London'. By 1543, records show it was quite extensively developed with a number of important houses, several churches and a landmark known as The Temple.

By the following century, the area next to Fleet Street and the Temple was known infamously as Alsatia and avoided by every right-thinking citizen. Protected by law as a sanctuary until 1697, it had become home to every kind of criminal, who could live there free from harm by the authorities. A Chief Justice going there once required a troop of musketeers for protection from the dangerous rabble who lurked at every corner.Today, the location of that Temple, which has given its name to the area at the top of Fleet Street which separates if from The Strand – the Temple Bar is marked by a memorial statue known as The Griffin, which divides the traffic near the junction with Chancery Lane. Prior to the erection of this striking sculpture of the winged creature from mythology, there had been, since at least the twelfth century, a demarkation line on the spot to mark the western boundary of the city of London. The very earliest 'bar' was no more than a chain hung between two posts and was probably erected by the Templars to indicate the extent of their lands at that time.

Later, actual gates were constructed across the road, and in the reign of James I a proper archway was built. In 1672 this Was replaced by a new Temple Bar of Portland Stone designed by Sir Christopher Wren which remained on the site until 1878. Then, due to the enormous increase in London's traffic which had made the spot terribly congested, it was decided to remove the archway. It was thereupon summarily sold to a London brewer who had it removed to the grounds of his home at Theobald's Park in Hertfordshire.

Though there can be no denying that the Temple Bar was a striking-looking construction and many Londoners were sorry to see it go, it had earned a rather sinister reputation which made it a place to avoid by night. For years, it was customary for the heads of executed criminals to be placed on iron spikes and stuck up on the top of the gateway. The English diarist and novelist, John Evelyn, who frequently had to pass this way called the Temple 'a dismal sight' and the array of traitors' heads upon it 'a revolting spectacle'.

Three heads which had been on the Temple since 1746 were still there when Sweeney Todd took up his residence just a stone's throw away. A curious contemporary print of these macabre relics and a description of two of the men who had lost their heads still exists. The picture is all the more curious because of the devil figure looking down in triumph and waving a banner on which are inscribed the words, 'A Crown or a Grave'.

Sweeney Todd would in all probability have known the history of two of the heads on the iron poles, those of Townley and Fletcher; but for the benefit of the reader let me quote this brief history from Walter Thornbury's excellent book, *Haunted London* (1880), which also reprinted the gruesome illustration:

'The heads of Fletcher and Townley were put up on Temple Bar on August 2, 1746. On August 16, Horace Walpole wrote to his friend Montague to say that he had "passed under the new heads at Temple Bar, where people made a trade of letting spy-glasses at a halfpenny a look".

'Townley was a young officer about 38 years of age, born at Wigan, and of a good family. He had been 15 years abroad in the French army, and was close to the Duke of Berwick when the duke's head was shot off at the seige of Philipsburgh. When the Highlanders came into England he met them near Preston, and received from the young Pretender a commission to raise a regiment of foot soldiers. He had been also commandant at Carlisle and directed the sallies from thence before his capture and trial.

'Fletcher, a young linen chapman at Salford, had been seen pulling off his hat and shouting when a sergeant and a drummer were beating up for volunteers at the Manchester Exchange. He had been seen also at Carlisle, dressed as an officer, with a white cockade in his hat and a plaid sash round his waist.

'Who the other Jacobite shown upon the Temple roof and most likely executed for treason with these two I have no idea.'

Perhaps not surprisingly, the heads often attracted the wrong kind of attention from people who went further than merely staring at them. In January 1766, for instance, a man was arrested for 'discharging musket-balls from a steel cross-bow' at the heads because he believed 'it was not sufficient that traitors should merely suffer death', Walter Thornbury tells us. While in April 1772 'one of the rebel heads fell down after a storm' and was quickly hurried away and sold as a relic in a nearby public house.

According to other sources, there were people still living in Fleet Street at the end of the nineteenth century who could remember seeing the decomposing heads hanging on the Temple Bar until they finally fell off into the street below. Indeed, the last of the iron spikes was not actually removed from the arch until the middle of the 1800s.

Fleet Street itself had been swallowed up in the sprawl of London by the sixteenth century, and its character and that of its residents had also changed rapidly. To be sure, there were still a number of fine buildings facing the street; but behind them where there had once been fields and gardens things were very different indeed. The area had, in fact, become one of lawlessness and debauchery, as this report from the year 1570 graphically illustrates:

'The poor watchmen of the parish of St Bride's, Fleet Street, being called forth on Thursday night (April 1570) to aid the sheriff in quieting a broil in Fleet Street, were all wounded, and are likely to be cripples for ever.'

In his definitive study of the area, *Annals of Fleet Street* (1912), E. Beresford Chancellor explains the reason for this change of character:

'The presence in the street of a large number of taverns had much to do with this state of affairs,' he wrote, 'and the defective means of policing the streets made it an easy matter for the lawless to perpetrate their daring deeds, and then to hurry off to the safe asylum of the contiguous byways and alleys, or to seek shelter in the wilds of Whitefriars.'

One of the most notorious drinking dens in London, the 'Devil's Tavern' was located at number 2 Fleet Street and records show it had been a noisy and unruly place since the time of James I. Curiously, not far away were the premises of a bookseller, William Owen, who combined this business with selling, 'German Spa Water from ye Pyrmont in their utmost Perfection, Bath, Bristol & Other English Waters fresh every week.' The importance of this trade was such that the illustration on Owen's card was of bottles not books. Certainly Fleet Street well deserved its reputation as a place for liquid refreshment of all kinds!

Mr Chancellor goes on to say that the Domestic State Papers are full of accounts of murders, robberies and thefts in Fleet Street during the times of the Tudors and their successors. Drawing a parallel with his own times, the author added, 'You might not incur the risk of being run down by a motor bus or taxi-cab, but you stood a very good chance of being dirked or clubbed if you were dissipated enough to be out of doors after, say, nine o'clock in the evening.'

But for those criminals who were caught, Mr Chancellor says, retribution was swift – for it was not unusual for a person to be promptly hung near the very scene of their crime. The sight of a gibbet newly erected bearing its latest grisly victim was not at all an unusual one to the people of Fleet Street. Indeed, a famous instance was still a popular topic of conversation when Sweeney Todd moved into the area.

The case, which happened in 1728, was all the more intriguing because the killer was a twenty-five-year-old woman, Sarah Malcolm, who had killed her mistress and two fellow servants. She had cut the throat of one of her victims and strangled the other two. What made

Sarah notorious was the fact that many people believed she was innocent and regarded her as something of a heroine. The famous painter Hogarth, in fact, visited the young woman in her cell and painted her portrait.

Whatever the public might have thought, nothing could save Sarah Malcolm from the gallows, and it was decreed that she should suffer her punishment at the scene of her crimes. To this end, she was hanged in Fleet Street at a point just between Mitre Court and Fetter Lane. Thousands crammed the area to see her last moments as she climbed onto the gallows, 'her cheeks painted in honour of the occasion' according to one contemporary account.

Significantly, Sarah's fame in the annals of crime might well be better known today but for the arrival in the vicinity just a short while later of Sweeney Todd . . .

The evil and insanitary dens behind the facade of Fleet Street were, hardly surprisingly, prime targets for both fire and plague. Records indicate that in the year 1625 alone, over 500 people in the parish died from cholera. The west side of Fleet Street – perhaps the poorest of all the districts – was also devastated by the Great Fire of London in 1666. Samuel Pepys noted in his *Diary* that he had seen the flames 'running downe to Fleet Street'. Although systematic rebuilding in 1677 made some difference to the neighbourhood – and by widening the thoroughfare the conditions were made generally less insanitary – there was still no shifting the criminal fraternity who were too firmly entrenched in their hideouts to be displaced by either disease or flames.

Despite these unruly elements, Fleet Street was nevertheless acting as a magnet to many Londoners, and by the eighteenth century some of its taverns were a favourite meeting place for the exchange of gossip and news. Indeed, it was in these places that the first 'news sheets' were written and the plans laid for London's first daily papers.

The great forerunner of the newspaper industry was the *Daily Courant* which appeared in 1702 published 'for E. Mallet against the Ditch at Fleet Bridge'. Within a few years it was to have several rivals all of whom would cluster nearby in Fleet Street. Several booksellers and publishers likewise chose to locate themselves here – including the notorious Edmund Curll who issued a string of pornographic works from his ostensibly inoffensive address, 'at the sign of the Dial & Bible, against St Dunstan's Church'.

It is perhaps just worth noting that today's visitor to Fleet Street seeking an example of the kind of atmosphere which nurtured this creativity can do no better than to visit the famous 'Cheshire Cheese' in Wine Court which, with its low-beamed rooms and sawdust-strewn wooden floors, is still redolent with the ghosts of its famous regulars like Dr Johnson, Addison, Boswell, Dickens, and many more.

A quite different sort of attraction for the ordinary men and women were the exhibitions and shows staged on Fleet Street, as E. Beresford Chancellor has also explained:

'The Eighteenth Century was the heyday of "shows" for which the thoroughfare became noted. The exhibition of monsters, contortionists, fire-eaters, waxworks and moving pictures were more to the taste of Fleet Street patrons than the concord of sweet sounds, or music married to immortal verse. Ben Jonson (in *Every Man in his Humour*) refers to "a new motion of the City of Nineveh, with Jonas and the whale" being exhibited at Fleet Bridge; and when he makes Knowell end a speech with the words, "Here within this place is to be seen the true, rare and accomplished monster, a miracle of nature," he is probably copying some such announcement seen by him in front of one of the Fleet Street shows.

'Nothing seemed then to come amiss to the curiosity of the public. It was as happy in looking at the giants striking the hours on St Dunstan's clock as in inspecting a model of Amsterdam "thirty feet long" or in regaling its sight on a legless child, measuring but eighteen inches, who was to be seen at a grocer's in Shoe Lane at the sign of the "Eagles and Child". All kinds of wonderful and fearsome animals attracted crowds, from a great Lincolnshire ox, nineteen hands high, to an old she-dromedary and her young one.'

'The Duke of Marlborough's Head at Shoe Lane seems to have been a great centre of attraction,' Mr Chancellor adds, 'for here, at various times, were exhibited a "moving picture"; "The Great Posture-Master of Europe" who "extends his body into all deformed shapes"; and a certain De Hightrehight who, besides eating burning coals, satisfied a curious appetite by sucking a red-hot poker five times a day. Automaton clocks and giants and dwarfs proved great "draws" – indeed Fleet Street was quite noted for the latter.'

Perhaps, however, the greatest of all the attractions in Fleet Street at this time was Mrs Salmon's Waxworks which drew thousands of curiosity seekers for over half a century. These figures had actually all been made somewhat earlier by the remarkable Mrs Salmon and exhibited in Aldersgate until her death in 1760 at the ripe old age of ninety. Thereafter they were purchased by a man named Clark who moved them into new premises at 189 Fleet Street, where they remained a constant source of amazement until 1812 when the whole collection was inexplicably broken up and sold. A handbill posted soon after the show arrived in Fleet Street is very illuminating:

The Royal Offspring: Or, the Maid's Tragedy Represented in Wax Work, with many Moving Figures and these Histories Following. King Charles the First upon the Fatal Scaffold, attended by Dr. Juxon the Bishop of London, and the Lieutenant of the Tower, with the Executioner and Guards waiting upon our Royal Martyr. The Royal Seraglio, or the Life and Death of Mahomet the Third, with the Death of Ireniae Princess of Persia, and the fair Sultaness Urania. The Overthrow of Queen Voaditia [Boadicea], and the Tragical Death of her two Princely Daughters. The Palace of Flora or the Roman superstition. The Rites of Moloch, or the Unliu-mane Cruelty, with the manner of the Canaanitish Ladies, Offering up their First-born Infants, in Sacrifice to that ugly Idol, in whose Belly was a burning Furnace, to destroy those Unhappy Children. Margaret Countess of Heningbergh, Lying on a Bed of State, with her Three Hundred and Sixty-Five Children, all born at one Birth, and baptized by the Names of Johns and Elizabeths, occasioned by the rash Wish of a poor beggar Woman. Hermonia a Roman Lady, whose Father offended the Emperor, was sentenced to be starved to Death, but was preserved by Sucking his Daughter's Breast. Old Mother Shipton the Famous English Prophetess, which fortold the Death of the White King; All richly dress'd and composed with so much variety of Invention, that it is wonderfully Diverting to all Lovers of Art and Ingenuity.

The impression left on visitors to Mrs Salmon's collection of 140 figures, famous and infamous, ancient and modern, can be judged from the recollections of a man who visited the show in 1793 and reported in another communication to *Notes & Queries* signed by a correspondent with the initials 'G.S.':

'I remember in the collection was a representation (and a horrible one it was!) of Ankerstrom stabbing the king of Sweden; also, the

Cherokee Chiefs and Renwick Williams, called the Monster, cutting up the Miss Porters & etc & etc. I was then quite a youth and the hideous copper countenance of the chiefs, together with the bloody appearance of the Swedish king, and the Miss Porters, contrasting so frightfully with the sweaty death-like faces of the principal figures, riveted the scene so firmly on my memory, that I have it now as fresh in my mind's eye as when I first held it, forty-four years since.'

Other visitors were also impressed – not to say startled – by receiving a farewell kick from the mechanised Mother Shipton as they prepared to leave and reenter Fleet Street. The exhibition was clearly a magnet for young and old – William Hogarth, for example, later wrote that when he was an apprentice he, 'frequently loitered at old Mother Salmon's, when I was sent of an errand into the city, to take a peep' – and it is inconceivable to me that Sweeney Todd would not also have paid a visit to his neighbour. His interest, though, might just have been more excited by another facet of Mrs Salmon's show. Richard D. Altick describes this in his panoramic history of *The Shows of London* (1978):

'The floor of the exhibition was booby-trapped with hidden treadles, which, when stepped on, not only set Mother Shipton kicking, but threw another figure into a threatening attitude with an uplifted broom.'

Is too much of a stretch of the imagination to suggest that this revolving machinery might not have planted the seed in Sweeney Todd's mind that later germinated into his death-dealing chair? Where other visitors had gone in for an hour or so of harmless amusement, the barber had seen an instrument that could be put to a much more sinister purpose? Is it not possible, too, that Mrs Salmon's customers might not have followed up their visit with a call to the nearby barber – though few would have had the opportunity to go in the opposite direction? We shall see.

This, then, was the locality in which Sweeney Todd decided to open his business in 1785. A little corner of London famous for its lawlessness and taste for the macabre. It was, in truth, ideally suited for a man with a taste for both – and was soon to combine them with deadly efficiency.

Easy Shaving For A Penny

Historians have had a lot of harmless fun over the years arguing about the exact address of Sweeney Todd's shop in Fleet Street. The debate has taken on something of the fascination of the search for 221B Baker Street, the famous address of London's greatest detective, Sherlock Holmes. The difference is that we *know* the Great Detective was fiction and his creator, Sir Arthur Conan Doyle, merely picked the address now occupied by the Abbey National Building Society because it was suitable for his purpose.

The various localities for the site where Todd hung out his sign, 'Easy shaving for a penny – As good as you will find any,' are, however, worth considering in connection with what occurred later during the barber's relationship with his partner-in-crime, Mrs Lovett.

In one of the earliest fictionalisations of Todd's life, *Sweeney Todd, The Demon Barber of Fleet Street,* written anonymously for the London publishing firm of Charles Fox in 1878, his address is given as 69 Fleet Fleet.

'If you have any wish to take a greater criminal than I,' Mrs Lovett told the Bow Street Runners upon her arrest, 'then go to the shop of one Sweeney Todd, a barber, in Fleet Street. His number is sixty-nine. Seize him and I shall be content.'

The choice of this number by the writer is curious and obviously inaccurate – for the address is actually towards the lower end of Fleet Street near Ludgate Circus, and contradicts all the known facts about which side of the street the shop was situated on by being on the opposite side of the road.

Nor is the evidence any better for another possible location, number 154 Fleet Street. This second number was cited in at least two letters about Sweeney Todd published in the scholarly magazine, *Notes & Queries,* during a debate concerning the Demon Barber in the 1890s.

When no reader could confirm or deny the claim, interest in the subject faded – and did not reappear until half a century later in 1947.

Then the matter came to public attention again as a result of some demolition work in Fleet Street during which a most surprising discovery was made. Let me quote from the report that appeared in the *London Evening News* of 24 April, 1947:

Cellars beneath St Dunstan's Church.

'Many people are loath to believe that Sweeney Todd was never more substantial than a legend. They are joined today by Alfred Waller, a burly builder's manager, who, hitherto, had no strong opinions on the matter.

'Mr Waller, who is at work on a building in Fleet Street, told me today he thinks he has discovered proof that number 154 – on the north side, opposite Bouverie Street – was the celebrated barber's shop.

The old number 154 is being demolished to make way for new premises. During his work on this enterprise, Mr Waller has found a fanlight and some pieces of wood which were buried below plaster, all bearing the Demon Barber's name.

'Signs of trap-doors, and a cellar with a manhole which leads to a sewer, lend substance to this belief.'

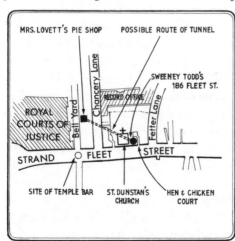

Sweeney Todd's secret route.

Much as many people must have hoped the claim could be substantiated, the explanation for the signs proved to be disappointingly prosaic. In fact, just prior to the Second World War an enterprising barber had occupied 154 and decided to cash-in on the fame of the Demon Barber of Fleet Street by calling his business 'Sweeney Todd, Barber'. It was, sadly, his old sign board that Mr Waller had uncovered.

In 1956 a similar story emerged in the pages of *The Story Paper Collector,* a magazine for those interested in the origins of working class and juvenile fiction. In an article about Sweeney Todd, contributor Charles W. Daniels had this to say:

'Some years ago I corresponded with a fellow collector who spent much of his spare time in literary research. In response to an enquiry, he sent me a foolscap sheet torn from a manuscript book. One side of the paper had a number of notes relative to the matter I had in hand . . . The other side contained items of information concerning various stories. I quote one: "Sweeney Todd. From an account published about the middle of the 18th Century. While an empty shop in Fleet Street was undergoing repairs the workmen discovered several bodies buried beneath the cellar flooring. The man who had occupied the premises had recently died. He was a barber named Todd." At the time I had no interest in this character, and now it is too late. Of course I am quite willing to admit that such evidence as this would carry little weight in a court of law, but it does seem to fit in with the observation of Summers about their being "a substratum of truth" in the story. Is it unreasonable to suppose that the "substratum of truth" is embodied in the above note? It would also explain why there are no official records of Todd, for you cannot put a dead man on trial for murder.'

The evidence in favour of 186 Fleet Street, beside St Dunstan's Church and standing in the shade of the site of the old Temple Bar, is, I believe overwhelming. Not least because of its position in direct line to Bell Yard on the other side of the church where the pie shop was placed, but even more so because of the many passageways and tunnels which had been discovered, providing a link between the two points.

The facts also concur with the description given in the first novelisation of the legend in *The String of Pearls* which appeared in *The People's Periodical* of 21 November, 1846, and to which we shall

round,' one incumbent wrote in the eighteenth century, 'there
...ps which cling barnacle-like to the south side and east front
...ing all sorts and descriptions of trades. There are many
...s in the vicinity used by lawbreakers and passages running
...round beneath them through which the thieves escape after ill-
...heir victims.'

...aze of small courts and alleyways in the vicinity also made it
...r the pick-pockets and petty crooks to disappear quickly with
...oils, as E. Beresford Chancellor has also written:

...e chief characteristic of the north side of Fleet Street is the
...r of small courts and alleys which, at that time, were found
...Some have disappeared, like the famous Johnson's Court, which
...sorbed in Aderton's Hotel. Some were but means of access to
...areas behind the houses in the main thoroughfare, and have
...e obliterated in the course of building developments. Not a few,
...er, still remain, and it is in these exiguous outlets that one can,
...nd there, best gain an approximate idea of what Fleet Street must
...ooked like to our fore-fathers.'

...t, Mr Chancellor adds succinctly, 'In the days of George the
..., the area was, quite simply, a hot-bed of lawlessness which the
...rities stood little chance of penetrating and rarely attempted to.'

...cording to one report, Sweeney Todd paid £125 for the lease of
...Fleet Street. His agreement was to pay an annual rental to the
...ers Company of £17.10s per annum and 'consenting to keep
...remises in ordinary repair'. Prior to his occupation, the shop had
...used by a hosier, but Sweeney converted the ground floor for use
...barber's and kept the upper floors for living accommodation. On
...ide of the house was a passage known as Hen & Chicken Court
...h lead into a labyrinth of passageways; while on the other a house
...pied by a shoemaker named Whittle.

...hen Sweeney Todd opened for business it was evident he had
...spent a great deal of time or money on preparing the premises.
...anonymous description written at the turn of the century
...ures a bunding that had probably changed very little in the
...rvening years.

...he evil-looking house looked as if it had been left there in the
...of the dark ages, and had missed the advancing hand of
...ization. Its blackened front, its windows shrouded with dirt and

be returning later for a fuller discussion. The opening paragraph of the
story reads:

'Before Fleet Street had reached its present importance, and when
George the Third was young, and the figures who used to strike the
chimes at old St Dunstan's Church were in all their glory – providing
a great impediment to errand-boys on their rounds and a matter of
gaping curiosity to country people – there stood close to the sacred
edifice a small barber's shop which was kept by a man of the name of
Sweeney Todd.'

There is factual evidence to back this piece of fiction, too. The
evidence has been brought to light by the historian and researcher W.
O. G. Lofts who has greatly assisted me in the research for this book.
According to Mr Lofts, during the 1880s, some very old buildings in
Fleet Street close to St Dunstan's Church were pulled down.
Underneath the cellars of number 186 a large pit of bones was found.
'At first these seemed undeniably like the remains of some of Sweeney
Todd's victims,' Mr Lofts says, 'but on closer investigation another
possibility became apparent. The old St Dunstan's Church which had
been rebuilt about 1830 used to stand east to west and so therefore the
bones under 186 could equally have been from the old church vaults.'
Indeed they could. But, as we shall see later, they could just as easily
have been the bones of some of Todd's victims hidden among older
relics to cover up the full enormity of his crimes.

During my research I also received a number of letters and
communications of support for my contention about this locality. One
of the most interesting letters was from Alan Pennie, an electrician
from Colchester in Essex, who had worked in the vicinity. He wrote
to me in May 2001:

'It is certainly difficult to work out exactly where the location of
Sweeney Todd's shop was. However, I have worked in the area of Fleet
Street where the story is set and it states that the cellar where the
chopping and baking were done was "of vast extent and sepulchral
appearance and may have extended right under Chancery Lane and
what is now the Law Courts Branch of the Bank of England." This
bank was extensively rebuilt on the inside and converted to a wine bar
for the Fuller Group.

'I was involved in the electrical installation and all the incoming
supplies were in the basement area which was confined to several old

bank vaults. The oldest part was a row of arches that extended under the road at the front – Fleet Street – *below* the level of the area. The gap between the building and the pavement was one floor down. The set of arches were much liker the ones in your photograph. (See art section.) They were bricked up towards the road so they must have extended further under it. Where, before the road was made wider, these vaults would have been under a building. There were several areas of large stone which must have been foundations for supporting walls before the Bank was built.'

Another correspondent, Ivy Bass of Baldock in Hertfordshire, added some further equally fascinating information with a rather chilling aspect to it. Her letter was written to me in November 1995:

'When I was a young girl in the early Twenties, I used to work at 184, Fleet Street. It was then the ABC Tearooms and I remember there was a tiny kitchen in the basement. Adjoining it was a very dark and horrid little yard. We girls always said that the place was haunted and we even called it "Sweeney's." We used to play tricks on new girls that came to the shop by dressing up as a ghost and springing out on them. I have thought about it all these years and I think 184 must have been next to Sweeney Todd's at 186.'

A third letter came from Roy Farrell in Pickering, North Yorkshire in February 2000. He was researching his family history and had discovered that his great-great-grandfather had owned 189, Fleet Street in the 1870's. He was not suggesting there might be a connection with the demon barber, he told me, but he felt sure I would be interested to know that the occupation of his relative, James Farrell, had been – hairdresser!

Then, just as I was completing this new edition, London filmmaker Tom Whitter got in touch with me and added yet another intriguing piece to the jigsaw. He had become fascinated by the legend and, in particular, the stories of passageways beneath St Dunstan's. He had managed to locate some old plans of the cellars and tunnels, wnich satisfied him that this labyrinth made communication between Fleet Street and Bell Yard perfectly feasible. He invited me to visit the underground chambers and it was not difficult to visualise how they might have served the purposes of Sweeney Todd and Mrs Lovett. Tom also explained that there were now CCTV cameras operating in a few of the larger chambers.

'The curious thing is,' he added, 'that eve has shown up on footage taken by the camera is – but it is certainly a mystery.'

'Could it be the ghost of Sweeney Todd? question hanging in the air . . .

* * *

St Dunstan's Church, which was to play such legend of Sweeney Todd, was one of the focal 1785 – as it remains to this day. Although a ch site since the thirteenth century, the present bu 1833. It is the previous edifice in which we are in projected further into the thoroughfare than the result of the Great Fire when the surrounding bu their previous line in order to give pedestrians an

The earlier St Dunstan's had a tower and a ba over the lower windows, but undoubtedly its mos a clock projecting over the street with two figures an alcove to strike each hour. Installed on the clock became one of the sights of London, not to The two life-like figures represented savages and 'Giants of St Dunstan's'. They were carved in armed with a club with which they struck each qu two bells suspended between them. As the figures their heads also moved from side to side.

This ingenious timepiece had been made by one Water Lane, London who apparently got £35 plus t job! By contrast, it is perhaps worth noting that wh pulled down in 1830 to make way for the new or Hertford who had been fascinated by the clock as a it for the princely sum of £210 and set it up agai Villa, Regent's Park.

Apart from the many sightseers that the cloc Dunstan's, it was also considered a fashionable chu indicate it was much used by the London gentr christenings and burials. None of this, though, prev from being constantly worried about the disorderly n which they were situated.

rubbish, and its beetling gables impressed those who saw it with feelings of foreboding.'

Todd had, though, advertised his dual role of barber and surgeon with a number of items on display at the shop. A long white pole striped with red projected from the front of the building, and over the door were painted in fat, yellow letters the words 'Sweeney Todd, Barber'. Behind the front windows, Todd arranged several wigs and perukes on blocks roughly shaped like heads. Beside these stood a number of jars filled with what was evidently coagulated blood and some bottles of rotten teeth. These were to advertise his skills at pulling teeth and bleeding clients for minor ailments. A solitary razor, open, hung in one panel of the window below a board proclaiming in rhyming doggrel, 'Easy shaving for a penny – As good as you will find any.'

Inside, the shop was no more impressive. Heavy beams seemed to bring the ceiling down, while the darkened walls only enhanced the general gloom of the place. Two oil lamps hanging on opposite sides of the room were normally only lit as evening began to fall. Underneath one of these on a peg hung a number of dirty-looking sheets, some spotted with blood, which the barber would place around the necks of his customers. A scarred and grimy bench ran the length of the back wall. On this Todd had arranged the tools of his trade including combs, brushes, shaving bowls, some hanks of hair and a number of sharp knives and pincers.

Above these items, neatly hanging in a row, were his collection of razors. Pride of place was given to a Magnum Bonum, made of the finest steel and generally regarded as the sharpest and most proficient of all razors. Sweeney Todd had apparently not chosen to renew his acquaintanceship with John Crook, the razor-maker to whom he had been apprenticed, but purchased three blades from Henry Patten in nearby Middle Row, Holborn. One of Pattern's business advertisements has survived and is reproduced in this book. Unfortunately, Middle Row, where his premises were located, was an island row of houses towards the south side of the street by Holborn Bars opposite the end of Gray's Inn Road, and it suffered a similar fate to Todd's barber shop. It was pulled down in 1867.

On the left hand wall of the shop a small fireplace burned lumps of coal to boil the water for shaving and the minor operations. Alongside it hung a leather strap on which the barber stropped his razors before attending to each customer. Alternately, he had a stone with which to grind the heavier blades.

The observant visitor might have noticed that the bare wooden floor of the shop bore a number of dark stains, especially around a large, old-fashioned chair standing in the middle of the room. This was made of carved oak and had ornate legs and a high back. But only the very keen-eyed would every have noticed how tightly it was screwed to the floor and the very tiny gaps forming a square around the legs. And by then it might well have been too late . . .

The barber himself was, if anything, even less attractive than his shop. Accounts describe him as a sullen looking figure, with heavy eyebrows, a hard mouth and generally pugnacious features.

'Sweeney Todd was a barber in a small way of business,' says an account published in the *Gentleman's Magazine* of 1853. 'He was always grumbling about how hard times were, dressed in the plainest of clothes and had all the appearance of being a poor man. But there was also something very sinister about him with his pale face and reddish hair. At times he was like some hobgoblin, his strange, dark eyes agleam with greed and cunning.'

Another account in *Reynold's Miscellany* of December 1848 was even less complementary, if a little fanciful: 'Sweeney Todd was a man of middle age, and so repulsive in appearance that it is a wonder that such stray customers who ventured into his shop did not immediately flee from it when the demon in human frame commenced operations. The glitter in his eyes was as keen as the razor he flashed and wielded with the dexterity of one skilled in his craft.

'He was a long, loose-joined, ill-shaped fellow, with a huge mouth filled with black teeth. His hands were of abnormal size, he had immense feet and wiry hair, sometimes bristling with the combs used in his trade. Sweeney Todd also squinted, and was as ugly a wretch as could be seen in a day's march. But people did not pay much attention to him, and let him go his own way, for he seemed a harmless, reserved man, aware of his looks, and consequently avoided the society of his fellow creatures.'

In the shop, the barber invariably wore an apron, keeping a pair of scissors in the pocket. Later it transpired that he also concealed a razor up his sleeve, 'a little habit of mine,' he once said, 'for living in a dangerous place like London.'

When Sweeney did venture out, it was usually on business to visit the houses of wealthier clients whom he would shave or attend to their perukes and wigs. For pleasure, he apparently visited the Bald-faced Stag, 'an evil-looking public house' in Fleur-de-Lis Court off Fetter Lane. Here he would only drink brandy – the memories of what gin had done to his parents haunted him all his life.

Sweeney Todd was clearly a man who kept himself very much to himself in the early period of his career in Fleet Street. Little was known about his habits or who he consorted with, although as time passed he began to be looked upon a little suspiciously, as the *Gentleman's Magazine* also makes clear:

'It was true that all sorts of unpleasant rumours and surmises began to be whispered regarding him, up and down the street; for several people – seafaring men – who had been last known to visit his shop had disappeared as completely as though the earth had opened and swallowed them – but no one could prove that he had anything to do with these disappearances.'

Indeed, this state of affairs was to continue for some years. But behind the shutters of 186 Fleet Street, the man who gave 'Easy shaving for a penny', was actually operating a most diabolical scheme of robbery and murder.

The Human Ghoul

The London of 1785 was an almost perfect environment in which a cold and calculating murderer might hope to profit from killing *and* escape detection into the bargain. Human life was held cheap, and for the majority of those dwelling in the city their lives were short, brutish and miserable in the extreme.

Drink was both the comfort and the cause of much of the unhappiness. Hogarth's famous painting of 'Gin Lane' with rows of drunken bodies lying in the streets, customers squabbling in the shops selling spirits, and a general air of decay, squalor, poverty, illness and debauchery accurately sums up the existence of the ordinary men, women and children at this time.

Crime and punishment went virtually unchecked, too. Just the year before, no less a person than the Prime Minister, Lord North, had been held up and robbed by a highwayman in Gunnersbury Lane. These 'knights of the road', who were as popular with the public then as film and rock stars are today, lead a dangerous and colourful life and were expected to thumb their noses at the law and meet their death on the gallows with a smile and a wave to the massed crowds. Despite the fact that over 250 highwaymen were caught and hung in the quarter of a century from 1750, their numbers, if anything, increased.

Punishment was meted out by the authorities with little rhyme or reason. In 1785 alone a total of ninety-seven people were executed, predominantly for minor offences, including a boy of nine accused of breaking a window and a father of eight children who was hanged for stealing a loaf of bread. Small wonder that amidst all the disturbances, immorality and crime on the streets of the city, Samuel Johnson could describe it as, 'London – the needy villain's general home!'

The fact that London was then at a peak of both crime and punishment makes it easier to understand how the odds were stacked in favour of the clever criminal avoiding arrest. Tongues might wag, accusing fingers might point, but justice was still blind in trapping those who were skilled at law-breaking. And this skill might consist of little more than an ability to run quickly or lie convincingly.

Fog, too, was a great assistance to the criminal fraternity. The city had been prone to fogs ever since the first coal fires had been lit there in medieval times – assisted by the fact that London lay beside a river. The whole metropolis and its people were helpless in the grip of these annual fogs and could do nothing to prevent or mitigate them. Sometimes they lasted for months, and it was not unusual for the city to be swathed in cloying billows of greyish-white smoke from November to March. John Evelyn paints a vivid picture of such a scene in one of his *Diary* entries:

'The horrid smoke obscures our churches and makes our palaces look old. It fouls our clothes and corrupts the waters, so that the very rain and refreshing dews that fall in the several seasons precipitate this impure vapour, which with its black and tenacious quality, spots and contaminates whatever is exposed to it.'

These terrifying blankets of fog in which it was barely possible to see a hand in front of your face, were ideal for the perpetration of murder and robbery, allowing the criminal to vanish as quickly as he had arrived. Many people were lost in fogs never to be seen again: some were clubbed down in the streets, others drowned in the murky waters of the Thames, still more swallowed up in the open sewers or the footings of new buildings. Hundreds died from the effects, either directly or indirectly: it was impossible to establish which.

Records show that these fogs were at their worst in the middle of the eighteenth century, one of the thickest on record occurring in 1772 while Sweeney Todd was serving his sentence in Newgate. Even behind bars, he was no doubt aware of the nightmare of fear, inconvenience and disaster that the fog caused to everyone living in the city.

Looking back on all these factors it is, indeed, easy to understand how, in the London of 1785, Sweeney Todd was able to begin and then carry on for so long and with such impunity his campaign of mass murder.

The barber did not work all alone in his shop in Fleet Street. Like all tradesmen, he employed an apprentice – and in his case several; all of who came into and went from his service with suspicious frequency.

The actual number of 'soap boys' employed by Todd is unknown, but it must certainly have approached double figures.

As an employer, Todd treated his apprentices with the same mixture of cruelty and indifference that he himself had received. He was abie to recruit 'soap boys' with ease from among the starving vagrants of the capital, or alternately those children from rural hovels whose parents had pushed them off to the city in the hope that it might offer a better means of sustenance. As the historian Dorothy George has explained:

'Thus many children were apprenticed simply as drudges – girls to the lowest conceivable grades of domestic service, boys as helpers at stables or pot-boys. Others were apprenticed to trades, many to bakers and weavers, but the commonest trades for boys seem to have been tailoring and shoemaking. There were also trades so unprofitable or disagreeable that only parish children or the children of the very poor were apprenticed to them. All, though, shared the common fate of being wholly at the whim and temper of their employers.'

The duties of a 'soap boy' were to heat the water his master used for shaving, to fill the soap bowls, to sweep hair from the floor, and generally to do as he was told; the slightest infringement would earn him a beating. Most soap boys were made to sleep on their employer's premises and were fed with the scraps from his table.

There is evidence that the first boy employed by Todd was a teenager named Thomas Simpkins. The confirmation of this is to be found in a poignant little document discovered among the Demon Barber's effects after his arrest. It takes the form of a bill from the Peckham Rye Asylum to which Todd appears to have confined the boy at some period in 1786. It seems hard to believe the reason for this incarceration was madness on the boys' part, and I suspect that he had become the first to realise just what Sweeney Todd was doing to his unsuspecting clients.

The document reads: 'Mr Sweeney Todd, Fleet Street, London. Paid one year's keep and burial of Thomas Simpkins, aged fifteen. Found dead in his bed after residing at the asylum ten months and four days.'

The various fictional accounts of Sweeney Todd's life make much of his ill-treatment of his various apprentices, but actual details about the boys, their names, ages and where they came from are scant.

Understandably, with no one to turn to and the ever-present threat of a beating – worse still, to be turned out onto the streets again – most kept their silence: a silence they were to carry to their unknown graves.

The second murder which can with some confidence be ascribed to Sweeney Todd was, like the earlier one at Hyde Park Corner, committed in the street. In fact, the evidence points to the conclusion that it was to be some months – perhaps even a year or more – before the Demon Barber began regularly robbing and killing behind his own shop door.

This new crime was every bit as audacious as the first, and can be seen to bear the barber's hallmarks though, as before, he is not named in the newspaper account of the murder. The clipping is taken from the *Daily Courant* of 14 April, 1785:

A CUT-THROAT BARBER

A horrid murder has been committed in Fleet Street on the person of a young gentleman from the country while on a visit to relatives in London.

During the course of a walk through the city, he chanced to stop to admire the striking clock of St Dunstan's Church and there fell into conversation with a man in the clothing of a barber.

The two men came to an argument, and of a sudden the barber took from his clothing a razor and slit the throat of the young man, thereafter disappearing into the alleyway of Hen and Chicken Court and was seen no more.

The locality is, of course, right next door to Sweeney Todd's shop, and one can only wonder today why – on the strength of the identification – the barber was not one of the first people to be questioned by the law. But we are talking about very different times and a very different law enforcement agency – of which more anon.

An apprentice was also killed by Todd at around this same time, though not a boy in his employment. According to a certain Arabella Wilmot who is quoted in the Charles Fox version of our subject's life, the barber was the last person known to have seen alive a boy who worked for her family.

'A short time ago,' she stated, 'an apprentice in the service of my father was sent to the West End to receive a considerable sum of money. He never returned with it, and from that day to this we have heard nothing of him, although from inquiries my father made he ascertained that the apprentice had received the money. He was last seen parting from a friend at the Corner of Milford Lane, saying that he intended to call upon Sweeney Todd the barber to have his hair cut. My father later called upon this Sweeney Todd who indignantly denied that such a person had ever called at his shop.

'A reward was offered to anyone who could provide information regarding the boy's fate, but no clue whatever could be obtained. Not even the remotest trace was found of the poor lad and his disappearance remains a mystery,' she added.

This killing – if we are satisfied that Todd was the murderer – was die first in which he made financial gain. It was also to provide the pattern which most of his later crimes would follow: that of the customer who entered his shop never to be seen again.

The death shortly after this of a pawnbroker named Joseph Hansbury is also attributed to Todd. Rumour said that the barber had visited the man's premises nearby in The Strand on a number of occasions to shave him, and that he had been there just a few hours before Hansbury's body was found, his throat cut, lying in a pool of blood in one of the upstairs rooms above the shop. The coroner, however, returned a verdict of 'temporary insanity' and the pawn-broker was buried without further ceremony.

A somewhat shady dealer in stocks, bonds and lottery shares at the Royal Exchange named Rheuben Marney also suffered the same fate. He, too, was believed to have conducted some business with the Fleet Street barber, and was found in his place of business with his throat open from ear to ear. But once again apparently no attempt was made to interrogate Todd according to the available evidence.

Only one more victim is believed to have been murdered by Sweeney Todd beyond the confines of his shop – a man named Tony Thong, a petty crook and embezzler whose body was found in Fleur-de-Lis Court. A description of his death (also from the pages of the *Daily Courant*) indicates that his end was brutal in the extreme.

'The throat had been slashed with a razor from one side of the neck to the other. The skull, too, was crushed in, and the brain had gushed out as a sharp implement had entered the head, and lay in thick clots, matting the surrounding hair together in clammy flakes.

'Blood had also oozed from the mouth and ears, and, in addition to all this, the spine was completely broken, as was evident from the way in which the dead man was doubled up, the back of his head and his heels being nearly together.'

According to gossip once again, Thong was said to have been seen in conversation with Sweeney Todd several times in the public house which gave its name to the Court; but there were no friends or relatives to pursue any inquiries and the hapless Thong was soon after confined to a pauper's grave.

Although, as we have seen, crime was rampant throughout London in 1785-6, this spate of murders in the neighbourhood of Fleet Street gave rise to the suggestion that a 'Human Ghoul' was preying on the vicinity: a kind of forerunner to the Victorian era's infamous 'Jack the Ripper'. Certainly there is circumstantial evidence of this name being bandied about in local gossip, but unfortunately there are no actual newspaper accounts which might be helpful in linking it to the deaths ascribed to Sweeney Todd. In fact, Todd may well not have been the 'Human Ghoul' of rumour at all – but the trail of death he had already left would certainly have qualified him for the epithet. The gossip might also have served as a warning to him that he was running an ever increasing risk of discovery killing this way in public view.

Whether this surmise is true or not, there is no doubt that Sweeney Todd never again murdered one of his victims in their homes or on the streets of London. In fact, the indications are clear that by now he had the wherewithal to kill and rob with greater certainty and security on his own premises. Sweeney Todd was now in possession of his infamous revolving chair.

9

A Victim of The Fatal Chair

There is only one authentic account of a victim being murdered in Sweeney Todd's revolving chair, although all the fictional lives and stage dramas about the Demon Barber contain their own colourful versions. The report in question, which I have endeavoured to reconstruct in the following pages, was made by a London night-watchman whose father had been killed by Sweeney Todd around the year 1798.

The authenticity for this report is to be found in a book entitled *A Gothic Bibliography* by Montague Summers, a mammoth and painstaking study of macabre literature and its origins published in 1940. Summers, a Roman Catholic priest, spent years investigating the legend of Sweeney Todd, in literature, plays and reality, and concluded in his work:

'It has been denied that there was any such barber's shop in Fleet Street and the idea that Sweeney Todd has a real original has been scouted, a little rashly it would seem, for the authors of these works were drawing upon a long-standing and obstinate, if possibly only an oral authority, since there persisted a very old Fleet Street tavern tradition (current before 1800) that such an individual as Sweeney Todd existed, and his story is only a little exaggerated.

'This may well be the case,' Summers continues, 'as curiously crimes have an odd habit of repeating themselves in various countries even in detail. The old watchman, outside the gate of St Bartholomew's Hospital, used to aver that his father had been murdered for his coin by Sweeney Todd about 1798.'

There are few hospitals in London with a more fascinating history than St Bartholomew's Hospital situated in West Smithfield, a few yards from Newgate Street. Founded in the Middle Ages, it rose to pre-eminence in the medical field despite the bizarre theories of some of its early physicians. Notable among these was John of Gaddesden, the court physician to Edward II, who apparently advised in cases of smallpox that the patient should be wrapped in red and everything about him had to be the same colour! He also prescribed for a disease of the body known as stone, which hardened the skin, a plaster of dung and a mixture of headless crickets and beetles to be rubbed over the affected parts.

Barts Hospital was another London building to benefit from the will of the Lord Mayor of London, Sir Richard Whittington, although the major reconstruction work on the property did not take place until the eighteenth century when the familiar quadrangle structure was built. A laboratory was also added in 1793. This same era saw the presentation to the hospital of two paintings by Hogarth based on patients he had studied in the hospital, 'The Pool of Bethesda' and 'The Good Samaritans', both of which still hang in the building today.

Though long famous for its care of the poor of London, night-watchmen were still necessary to guard the premises after darkness, especially because of its proximity to Newgate Prison. In the later half of the eighteenth century, a number of hand-picked men were employed in this capacity. One of their small number was John Shadwell, the man whose father's throat had been cut by Sweeney Todd. The older Shadwell had been one of the seven Beadles employed by the hospital as a petty officer responsible for keeping law and order; and he had been able to use his position to secure his son work on the staff.

Shadwell's account of his father's murder has survived in an incomnlete handwritten document and in the oral traditions of West Smithfield, to which Montague Summers referred. I have here, though, attempted to put the facts together into narrative form.

* * *

It was a dark, rainy afternoon in late autumn as Thomas Shadwell made his way along Fleet Street to his job as a Beadle at St Bartholomew's Hospital. He lived in Covent Garden and normally walked the mile from his home by way of Temple Bar, down Fleet Street and Farringdon Street, and then up Snow Hill to the hospital. Normally he worked during the day; but the rising tide of crime in the city of late had made the hospital authorities concerned for security and they had instructed Shadwell to be doubly vigilant. He had therefore decided to work the occasional night shift.

Shadwell was a comfortably-off man, and took pride in his job and his appearance. He wore with care the three-cornered hat and cloak of his office which was provided by St Bartholomew's and he was always well turned out and clean shaven. In his pockets he always kept some change for a drink on his way home.

This day, however, his beard was feeling decidedly rough and he decided to have a shave before starting work. He had passed the shop with 'Sweeney Todd, Barber' over the door many times, but never ventured inside. Previously he had always gone to a barber he knew in Drury Lane, but today he felt like a change. It was to prove a fatal mistake.

As he neared Temple Bar, Shadwell became aware of how few people were about. Those like him who had to brave the elements were pressing as close to the buildings as they could to escape the worst of the weather. Although it was not yet quite five o'clock, the general gloom made it seem like evening already. It was going to be a long, wet night, Thomas Shadwell thought.

Lights were visible in the windows of most of the taverns and shops he passed, but it was only when a door was hastily opened by someone going in or out that any flash of colour and warmth illuminated the road outside.

In the downpour, the outlines of the buildings all around seemed indistinct, and the few people about huddled shapelessly into their clothes as they hurried by. There was not much traffic, either, and even the usual street sellers who peddled their wares had disappeared into the alleyways or taverns.

Shadwell paused just as he reached St Dunstan's Church. A whirring sound had caught his ear, and as his eyes glanced upwards at the big clock projecting from the side of the church, he saw the hour was just about to strike. For a moment there was stillness and then two small doors opened beside the clock face. A pair of gold-painted figures emerged, their heads moving from side to side. With mechanical efficiency they struck five blows on the bells suspended between them. Shadwell allowed the rain to drizzle onto his face as he watched. The sight of the clock in operation never failed to impress him, though he must have seen it a thousand times.

It was the flash of something from the nearby window of a shop which disturbed his thoughts. A flash of something silver illuminated by an oil lamp. It had come from the window of 'Sweeney Todd, Barber'.

The shop was ominously dark and evil-looking, Shadwell had decided on past occasions as he walked by; and on a day like this with the overhanging gabies throwing everything beneath into even deeper shadows, it looked, if anything, more sinister still.

The Beadle ran his hand over his chin. It was definitely heavy with stubble: he couldn't turn up for work like this. He shrugged. What shop in this grimy city didn't look the worse for wear after some of the bad winters there had been recently? he thought.

Shadwell made up his mind. He pushed open the door and walked into the barber's shop.

The man he saw standing inside in the feeble glow of a pair of oil lamps seemed very much what one would expect from the outside of his premises. He was heavily-built, had small, glinting eyes and a mouth with a rather unpleasant droop to it. His hair grew thickly on his head, and behind both ears he had a pair of combs. His hands were large, and his finger nails rather dirty, When the man smiled his ingratiating smile it became something akin to a squint.

For a moment, Thomas Shadwell stood rooted to the spot. The barber put down the razor he had been stropping and crossed the room to his side. Todd indicated the big wooden chair standing in the centre of the shop.

'Is it a shave you require, sir?' he said. 'Sit down. I'll soon polish you off.'

Shadwell then became aware of another, smaller, figure standing in the gloom. He made out the features of a young boy wearing an apron similar to that of the barber. He was obviously the man's 'soap boy'.

As if suddenly becoming aware of the boy, too, the barber spoke to him. 'Now, lad, I've just realised the time. I want you to hurry off and fetch me some fish for my tea while I attend to this gentleman. Here is the money. Now be off with you.'

The boy seemed to hesitate momentarily before taking the two coins from his master's outstretched hand. But once he had taken them, he hurried out of the front door without a backward glance.

Shadwell felt just the smallest twinge of unease as he allowed himself to be led to the chair: it was made of very sturdy wood, he thought, and he wondered why it was set in the centre of the room so far away from the table on which the barber kept his soap bowls and razors.

As he took off his cloak and hat and handed them to the barber whom he assumed must be the curiously named Sweeney Todd, Shadwell was conscious of the rain beating with increasing force against the window and the sound of some rusty hinges swinging to and fro outside.

'What a day it is, Mr Todd,' he said. 'I hope you have a steady hand.'

'Oh, don't be afraid of that, my dear sir,' the barber replied with something close to a smirk on his face. 'My hand is as steady as it was twenty years ago when I was a boy. The elements have no effect upon me, I assure you!'

At this he gave a sinister, rather mirthless laugh which made the hairs on the back of Thomas Shadwell's neck stand up.

'Do seat yourself comfortably, sir.' Sweeney Todd continued, taking down his Magnum Bonum razor and strapping it carefully on the belt hanging beside the fireplace.

As he settled back in the chair, Shadwell was conscious of a smell – a rather unpleasant smell. He was just about to sniff again, when the barber spoke.

'I have not seen you before, sir,' the tradesman said, finishing his stropping and now poised above his customer. 'I can see you are a man of distinction. A Beadle, too.'

'Indeed,' Shadwell replied. 'I am employed by St Bartholomew's Hospital. A fine hospital. Do you know it?'

'I have not had the need of its services,' the barber grinned his evil grin again, 'but I have heard good reports. You have an important position there?'

Shadwell could not resist preening himself.

'I am the most senior of the Beadles,' he said. 'Thirty years service. This fine timepiece was given to me only last year.'

The Beadle put his hand into his pocket and withdrew a gold watch on a chain that glinted in the light of the oil lamp. Some coins also jingled in his pocket as he moved.

'A fine piece. A fine piece, *indeed*,' the barber said, the gleam in his eyes hidden as he moved around to the back of the chair. Then:

'Oh, pardon me, sir. What am I thinking of. About to shave you without hot water! Do excuse me a moment while I go to my back room for a bowl and some more clean towels.'

Sweeney Todd instantly left the room. Shadwell allowed his eyes to roam around the place. It did not look as if it had been properly cleaned for years. Should he take this moment to get up and leave before this unsavoury man got to work on him? Polish him off, hadn't he said. After all, why should he pay to be frightened half to death?

The Beadle's thoughts were suddenly interrupted by a sound from the back room where the barber had disappeared. It sounded like the noise of a heavy bolt being drawn, followed by a noise of creaking that seemed to come from beneath his feet.

Before the startled man could even move, however, he felt the chair beneath him begin to tip backwards. The floorboards in front of his feet also started to rise up in front of his startled eyes, and an involuntary cry sprang from the lips. Then the ceiling seemed to spin before the Beadle's eyes and the last thing Thomas Shadwell ever felt was falling backwards out of his chair and plunging down, down into a stygian darkness . . .

Scarcely had the victim of Sweeney Todd's chair struck the floor of the cellar below with a sickening crunch and lapsed into instant unconsciousness, than another chair had revolved noiselessly to take the place of the original.

From behind the door, the Demon Barber peered into the room to assure himself that everything was as it should be. The shaving chair was once more empty awaiting the next customer.

Sweeney Todd selected one of his Patten razors from the rack on the wall and began to descend the stairs to his cellar.

'Another rich one for the picking,' he smirked to himself. 'See how I polish 'em off!'

* * *

The murder of the Beadle Thomas Shadwell remained undiscovered for two years until Sweeney Todd was finally arrested. The crime was not detected sooner not least because Shadwell had never used the barber's shop before and had never given anyone a clue that he might do so. Shadwell's son was sure his father had died in the barber's infamous chair because the old man's watch, his pride and joy, was later recovered from a cupboard at 186 Fleet Street. But of Shadwell himself not so much as a hair from his head was ever found.

There have been several suggestions as to how Sweeney Todd devised his 'fiendish weapon of death' as the shaving chair has been described. One unlikely account appeared in a leaflet, *Sweeney Todd, The Demon Barber,* written by Felix McGlennon in 1911.

'A conversation with a skilful mechanic gave him the idea of the trap-door,' McGlennon's account claims, 'which they made between them. And when it was completed Sweeney tested its efficiency upon the unsuspecting mechanic, and thereby became the sole possessor of the secret.'

This is not a theory which matches the facts, however. According to John Shadwell, when Todd was arrested he claimed to have invented the chair himself, utilising the skills of basic leverage which he had learned while apprenticed to the cutler: the purpose of the movable chairs, Todd claimed, was no more sinister than to allow him to easily tip away hair clippings and similar debris from his work directly into the cellar below!

In an authoritative article, 'Secret Hiding Places,' in the *Strand* magazine in December 1894, historian James Scott examines several examples of revolving chairs. He believes that each has been an updating of a type first developed in the Seventeenth Century to hide

The operation of Todd's chair.

royalist supporters of King Charles from Oliver Cromwell's pursuing Roundheads. If taken unawares by the approach of the enemy, these noblemen could instantly drop into a secret hiding place where a soft landing place had already been prepared. He writes:

'A notable feature of this invention is that, should the searchers suspect the existence of the trap-door, they would be greatly deceived in their endeavours to find it, the replacement chair fitting so closely as to conceal any connection with the space beneath the floor. Allowance is also made at the ends of the skirting for this curious mechanism which is motivated in spaces built in adjacent walls.'

Scott's statement is wholly valid. But it is to be regretted that such an expert knew nothing of the mechanical devices operating in Mrs Salmon's nearby waxwork exhibition that – in my opinion – may have been a more probable source of inspiration for that deadly chair in Fleet Street.

As the diagram here shows, the apparatus actually consisted of two chairs fixed onto opposite sides of a square section of floor-boards pivoted in the middle. A movable bolt fitted beneath the edge of these boards was joined by a system of rods to a small lever behind the rear door of the shop. By pulling this lever, the rods withdrew the bolt and the weight of the customer leaning back in the chair was sufficient to cause the contrivance to turn through forty-five degrees, so depositing the victim onto the stone floor below and the lower chair up into the shop. By returning the bolt to its former position, the chair was once more securely in place until required again.

The system was, in fact, simplicity itself – but deadly efficient.

Another statement Felix McGlennon made about the *modus operandi* of the Demon Barber is more accurate.

'Sweeney Todd made the discovery, perhaps by accident, that beneath his shop and the adjoining church were extensive underground passages and vaults stretching away in various directions, which few people had ever heard of or suspected to exist.

'Using the chairs he worked cautiously, murdering many, and grew rich, but the disposal of the bodies troubled him, as he had to bury them beneath the stones underground,' the report adds.

Sweeney Todd was certainly an ingenious and vengeful man; but he was also greedy and cunning. Not satisfied with the money and valuables he had already amassed, the barber sought for a better means of disposing of the troublesome bodies of his victims. He found the solution with the help of a woman whose name and gruesome reputation is now as much a part of the legend of the Demon Barber as his own.

10

The Secret of The Meat Pies

Not every customer that Sweeney Todd dispatched into his cellar died immediately they struck the ground. According to the *Gentleman's Magazine* version of his life, the chair killed outright five out of every seven victims, breaking their necks as they fell backwards onto the stone floor. The remaining few who showed any signs of life after their fall, Todd had to 'polish off by cutting their throats. The Demon Barber was always quick to inspect any body immediately after he had made sure that the chair was back in place. He would then slice through the jugular of his victim with practised ease.

The one problem that always remained after robbing the corpse was to dispose of it. Initially, there had been space in the underground vaults beneath the church which adjoined his cellar. But as the numbers mounted – and the work of burying the bodies became increasingly arduous – the killer sought for an easier alternative.

C. W. Biller, the author of *The Story of Sweeney Todd*, published in 1924, provides the basic details of the solution he found.

'Sweeney Todd had been intimate with a Mrs Lovett for some time when he discovered that a passage could be made to communicate with a shop in Bell Yard, and he installed her in it as an expert pie maker. Then the horrible idea occurred to him that it would be both profitable and expedient if she used the flesh of the dead for her pies, and if any of their assistants suspected anything – they, too, became pie fillings.'

Bell Yard, like Fleet Street, also enjoyed a notorious reputation at this period in history. Sir John Fortescue, the friend of the poet Alexander Pope, who once lived in a house in the cramped little passageway, referred to it derisively as 'that filthy old place'. Nonetheless, it obviously had a kind of charm and atmosphere of its own – an atmosphere which appealed to Charles Dickens, for one, because he placed part of his novel *Bleak House* (1852-3) in the vicinity. The chapter, "Bell Yard" gives an authentic account of the place as it must have looked at the time. Today, Bell Yard is a little haven of quiet running between the bustle of The Strand alongside the Royal Courts of Justice to Carey Street.

The information we possess about the Mrs Lovett who became Sweeney Todd's accomplice in crime varies considerably in the different versions of the legend. Some describe her as a middle-aged woman, rather plain, with a cold and uncomfortable smile; while others like the anonymous author of *Sweeny Todd, The Demon Barber* in the 1936 'True Crimes Series' published by C. Arthur Pearson present her as something of a beauty:

'She was tall and slender with a mass of dark curling hair and the golden, peachlike complexion of the true brunette. Her lips were vividly crimson, her long heavily lashed eyes of a dark green hazel, flecked near the pupils with little specks of gold. She carried herself with the half insolent air of one who was fully aware of the value of her own beauty, and her voice when she spoke matched her appearance and possessed a surprisingly cultured accent.'

If, as I suspect, such accounts rather over-glamourises Mrs Lovett, there is still plenty of evidence that she was attractive to men. For there had been more than one man in her life before Sweeney Todd appeared and changed her existence for ever.

The suggestion has been put forward that she had a penchant for strong, even violent men, and that this was the basis of her relationship with the barber. Yet just how she fell in with his appalling plan to use the bodies of his victims as filling for her pies is still a matter of debate.

There is also some disagreement among those who have studied the legend as to whether her Christian name was Margery or Sarah, as both appear in the various version of the story. As Margery is the most frequently used, it is the one I have settled for in these pages.

Mrs Lovett was apparently born in London, although nothing is known of her early history. In her teens she married a baker named Joe Lovett and for some years the pair ran a business in Holborn. After her husband's sudden and unexpected death, she is believed to have lived with a 'Major Barnet' until he was proved to be a fraud and had to flee the city. She was then for a time the mistress of a city merchant who installed her in a house in Covent Garden.

Her first meeting with Sweeney Todd is said to have taken place a few years after he had settled in Fleet Street when his nefarious activities had already made him quite wealthy. Still anxious to make more money, he was always on the look-out for new opportunities and apparently sensed something of a kindred spirit in Mrs Lovett's calculating eyes. The attraction between the big, ugly man and the buxom young widow was also, without doubt, strongly sexual.

The Charles Fox version of the Sweeney Todd story also confirms that the barber was the owner of Mrs Lovett's pie shop in Bell Yard.

'Sweeney Todd felt himself quite at home in Bell Yard,' the narrative states. 'He was, in truth, the landlord of Mrs Lovett's house. It had not been safe to make the extensive underground alterations in the place if Mrs Lovett had been the tenant of a stranger. So Sweeney had purchased the freehold.'

Felix McGlennon adds a little further interesting information about the nature of their relationship.

'Mrs Lovett was his mistress and partner in crime, but no one ever saw them together, for they met by means of mysterious underground passageways entirely unknown to the outside world. By a passage known only to himself and his paramour, Sweeney Todd could make his way towards the pie shop, and manipulating a secret spring he caused the wall to open like a door so he could enter the bakehouse.'

It was not uncommon in London in the eighteenth century for bakeries to be situated in the cellars of bread and pastry shops. A contemporary description of an establishment which was probably very similar to that of Mrs Lovett's, describes such underground bakeries as having rough red tiles on the floor and pieces of flint and ragged stones hammered into the earthen walls to reinforce them. Extra strength was provided by beams of timber in the ceiling propped up by wooden pillars set into the floor. A large furnace provided the heat for the ovens to cook the trays of pies, which were normally made in batches of a hundred. Once cooked, the pies would be transported to the shop above on a movable platform raised by a series of pulleys.

Thomas Peckett Prest, a contributor to the legend only a few years after the events who we will meet shortly, actually worked in Fleet Street and was familiar with Bell Yard. His description of Mrs Lovett's pie shop and its customers – predominantly clerks and lawyers from

Lincoln's Inn and Grays Inn as well as employees of the legal profession from Chancery Lane and HoJborn – can be taken as accurate and authentic.

'On the left hand side of Bell Yard, going down from Carey Street, was, at the time we write of, one of the most celebrated shops for the sale of veal and pork pies that ever London produced. High and low, rich and poor, resorted to it; its fame had spread far and wide; and at twelve o'clock every day when the first batch of pies was sold there was a tremendous rush to obtain them.

'Their fame had spread great distances, some even carried them into the country as a treat to their friends. Oh, those delicious pies! There was about them a flavour never surpassed and rarely equalled; the paste was of the most delicate construction, and impregnated with the aroma of delicious gravy that defied description; the fat and the lean meat were also so artistically mixed.'

The counter in Mrs Lovett's shop was horseshoe-shaped and it was the habit of some of the customers to sit around this while they ate and exchanged banter. Some were even said to have flirted with the owner, but her only encouragement had been to urge those who had any money left to buy more pies. There were those among her customers who said that her smile was only on her lips and not from her heart. She was a deceiver, a woman with a secret. Margery Lovett only had eyes for business, they maintained.

Certainly Mrs Lovett made good use of the money that came into her possession. Her love of expensive items inspired her to furnish the upper rooms of the shop with fine furniture and carpets, and it was whispered that her bed was covered with silken sheets. The irony of making love on the very material that had helped support his family would probably not have been lost on Sweeney Todd.

After their moments of intimacy – which legend tells us followed a successful murder and the preparation of the flesh for the meat pies – Mrs Lovett may well have found her lover's general coarseness and lack of education irritating. Indeed, she more than once complained about Todd's 'greed for money' when they already had more than enough to satisfy their needs. Margery Lovett considered herself an educated and clever woman and desperately wanted to broaden her knowledge of art and literature. She was, as another contemporary report put it, 'no common, everyday sort of woman'.

The Demon Barber, on the other hand, simply wanted to satisfy his lust for killing and his passion for money.

* * *

Sweeney Todd's skill at cutting up and dismembering the bodies of his victims has never been in question. He had learned the basic skills of the 'barber surgeon' from his first instructor, Plummer, and in the cellar beneath the shop perfected his ability with the regular practice each of his victims provided.

The speed with which the Demon Barber dismembered his victims before *rigor mortis* could set in and make his job so much more difficult says a lot about his expertise at this grim task. He had to work in the claustrophobic conditions of the tiny cellar with only a wax candle to provide illumination. With the amount of blood that must have spilled from the corpses onto the cellar floor, it is not difficult to imagine how slippery and unpleasant the whole place must have become. Sweeney Todd, apparently, never let such inconveniences bother him.

Once the bodies had been stripped of their clothes, Todd would butcher off the arms and legs and then slice the soft flesh from the torso. This would be added to the 'meat' stripped from the limbs plus the heart, liver and kidneys, and put in a box for carrying to Mrs Lovett's underground bakery. When he had separated up all the flesh that might be edible, he would make a separate pile of the bones and then carry them off into the adjacent vaults for disposal. In carrying out this part of his mission, the killer only had the light of his wax candle to guide him along the narrow passageways. Later evidence was to reveal that he had carefully picked a vault to hide the bones in which belonged to a local family named Weston whose line had many years earlier become extinct. It was one vault that was unlikely ever to be disturbed. There is a possibility that some of the other family tombs beneath St Dunstan's were used for this purpose, but only one description has survived of what was found in the Weston vault. It does not make pleasant reading.

'Piled one upon each other on the floor and reaching half way up to the ceiling, lay a decomposing mass of human remains,' the report from the *Daily Courant* says. 'Heaped one upon another, heedlessly tossed into the disgusting heap any way, lay pieces of gaunt skeletons with pieces of flesh here and there only adhering to the bones. Heads in a similar state of decay were tumbled about, the whole enough to strike such horror into the heart of any man.'

Successfully having concealed the bones in the vault, Sweeney Todd then carried the flesh along to Mrs Lovett's bakehouse, where it would be turned into the meat pies which she sold to her unsuspecting customers.

The various accounts of the Demon Barber's life are uncertain as to whether Mrs Lovett was solely responsible for preparing the pies. It is difficult to believe that she could have coped with her extensive clientele on her own; and one must not forget the claim in C. W. Biller's account written in 1924 that if any of the couple's 'assistants' suspected what was going on, 'they, too, became pie fillings'.

There is some evidence that Mrs Lovett employed a young girl to help her serve in the shop. Several of the fictionalised biographies also claim that she employed a pie-maker in the underground kitchen below. This is certainly feasible; and it is not beyond the realms of possibility that an uneducated man would have been unable to tell the difference between animal meat and that of human beings which had been sufficiently carved up. What makes it difficult to sustain this hypothesis is the complete absence of such a witness at the subsequent trial of Sweeney Todd. This, though, did not prevent the early chroniclers of the legend from introducing a cook who prepared the 'cannibal pies'. The anonymous author of *A Life of Sweeney Todd* (1897) even turned the pie-maker into the hero of his account as the man who ultimately exposed Mrs Lovett's evil trade.

'There was an awful stillness in the shop,' he writes, 'and all eyes were fixed upon Mrs Lovett and the cavity through which the next batch of those delicious pies were coming. The platform could be heard to be making its way upwards by means of a ratchet-wheel and catch.

'For a moment Mrs Lovett paused to take breath. The load seemed heavier than usual, she thought, or else her nerves were beginning to fail her. She began to turn the windlass again. At last the tops of the pies appeared.

'Those clustered in the shop saw the rim of the large tray, and just as the platform was level with the floor, up flew the trays and pies, as if something had exploded beneath them. A tall, slim man sprang out of the shaft and onto the counter.

'It was the cook who, from the cellar beneath, had laid himself as flat as he could beneath the tray of pies and so had been worked up to Mrs Lovett's shop.

' "Gentlemen," he cried, "I am Mrs Lovett's cook. The pies are made of *human flesh!*" '

Such a scene obviously made an ideal cliff-hanger for a Victorian penny dreadful, but the manner in which the conspiracy between the pie-maker and the Demon Barber was actually revealed began much more prosaically than that. The credit, in fact, belongs to an unpleasant smell and the relentless pursuit of a Bow Street Runner who picked up the scent.

The Bow Street Runners On The Scent

In the middle of the eighteenth century the state of Jaw enforcement, such as it was, meant that the clever criminal in London had a very good chance of escaping detection – not just once, but as often as his wits and ingenuity would allow him to keep one step ahead of those who represented the law.

It is a curious fact of British history that the people of these islands steadfastly rejected the idea of a 'police force' for generations. While every other country in Europe had its own professional law agencies, the very idea of the term police – a French word that first came into common usage in 1714 – seemed to Britons a threat to their freedom and individual liberties.

Across the Channel, the French had had a police force as long as their standing army. Both were expected to guard the frontiers against invasion; but when no such danger threatened, these 'police' men were expected to enforce the domestic laws. Not surprisingly, they were known as *gens d'armes* (men of arms) or *gendarmes*. Oliver Cromwell had actually made an attempt to introduce such a force in England – but it was at a time when his grip on the nation was slipping and the plan came to nothing. The whole concept seemed somehow 'un-English'. Even though highwaymen were robbing travellers on the country roads with seeming impunity, and burglars and footpads plagued those who lived in the towns and cities, still the business of enforcing the law was left almost solely to private enterprise. Those members of the public who did complain to the Houses of Parliament about the lawlessness of the country were brushed aside with the reply that it was the responsibility of the various country districts (the 'hundreds' which have since become modern parishes) to administer justice. In any event, they argued, it would be so costly to the exchequer to set up a professional force that it might well ruin the economy.

In effect, every man had to be his own policeman. Any person who was robbed was expected to raise the hue and cry and try to catch the criminal himself. If he was successful and wished to prosecute, he had to do so at his own expense. Small wonder that if the amount stolen was small or the criminal seemed a dangerous villain, few members of the public were prepared to play amateur detective.

Many of the officials of the hundreds had, however, made some kind of an attempt to preserve law and order by appointing parish constables, whose assistance any aggrieved person might enlist. But these men were all amateurs, doing their police work in their spare time: that many of them tackled the job with less than enthusiasm may be gauged by the fact that the job was compulsory and unpaid – not unlike jury service today. The term of office of these constables was for one year, and there is plentiful evidence that many a tradesman saddled with the job would pay – or even coerce – an employee to serve in his place. All constables were, though, entitled to charge a member of the public for their services.

There was another layer of authority above parish constables: the magistrates. They were unpaid also, although they were allowed to keep certain of the fees and fines they imposed. These men could order arrests and examine prisoners before they were taken to court. Many sat as judge and jury on the bench, too.

In fact, it was only in London that there was anything approaching a 'police force' before the mid-1800s. These were the band of night-watchmen who had been established in the second half of the seventeenth century during the reign of Charles II. Nicknamed 'Charlies', the job of these men was to patrol the streets at night, armed with a cudgel and a rattle with which to attract attention when any crime was discovered. These ostensibly 'professional' policemen were paid one shilling per night. The basic flaw in this arrangement was that the watchmen were mostly elderly men who had been unable to get work in the more strenuous professions: they were often scarcely able to lift a stick, let alone wield it! Consequently, most 'Charlies' were treated with brutality by the criminal fraternity if they interfered, and with scant regard by the general public.

In 1749, however, just seven years before Sweeney Todd was born, the first serious attempt to combat crime in London was initiated with the founding of the Bow Street Runners, Britain's first police-detectives. This famous band of men to whom we owe the modern Metropolitan Police Force, came into existence thanks to an unpaid Westminster magistrate named Colonel Thomas de Veil. Though not above taking bribes to line his own pocket, de Veil was a brave and energetic man who, without any assistance, carried out his own detective work to bring a large number of criminals to justice. At the end of his career he claimed, perhaps somewhat exaggeratedly, to have 'executed or transported over 1,900 of the greatest malefactors that ever appeared in England'.

De Veil's pioneer work was taken up by Henry Fielding, the novelist and author if *Tom Jones* (1749), who, uncertain of his success as a writer and anxious to secure the future for his family, accepted a magistrate's job with an annual guarantee of perks worth £1,000. Having weighed up the size of the problem he had inherited from de Veil, Fielding managed to persuade a group of six 'honest and true' former parish constables to band together and clear the London streets of criminals. Though he was in no position to offer them a salary, he would ensure the six received any rewards on offer.

Fired on by Fielding's own enthusiasm, these men – 'Mr Fielding's People' as they were first called – took to the streets to wage war on crime. Within two years, their number had risen to eighty and they were being called the Bow Street Runners, after the house in Bow Street where their chief lived.

The public were not charged for asking the Runners to investigate a crime, and everyone was encouraged to report cases of law-breaking to Bow Street. Tragically – and with his plans working so well – Henry Fielding died in 1754; but his place was at once taken by his equally-dedicated half-brother, John. John Fielding went on to expand the force with foot patrols; open a criminal records office; and launch a weekly journal of news and information about crime, *Hue and Cry,* which would later become the famous *Police Gazette.* He also gave the Runners their famous motto, 'Quick Notice and Sudden Pursuit'.

By 1792 the Bow Street Runners had a total of eight offices in the city, each with three salaried police-magistrates and six detective officers. The Runners were paid a salary of 25 shillings per week which served as a retaining fee: they also received a share in any reward when a criminal was caught and convicted. The best of these men might hope to earn several hundred pounds a year. Unlike the modern policeman, the Runners had no uniform – a state of affairs which did not change until 1805 when a standardised dress of blue coat and trousers, red waistcoat and black hat was chosen to make them look as little like soldiers as possible.

One of the busiest of these Bow Street Runner offices was situated at number 10 Craven Street, a major road just off The Strand running down to the banks of the Thames. The area of jurisdiction for this office extended from St James's Park to St Paul's Cathedral, and included the notorious Fleet Street.

It was to this office, and to its police-magistrate, Sir Richard Blunt, that the first stories of the unpleasant odour at St Dunstan's Church were conveyed in 1799. Thereby started the chain of events which would bring an end to Sweeney Todd's reign of terror.

* * *

Like the story of the Bow Street Runners themselves, there is very little factual evidence to draw upon about the career of Sir Richard Blunt. The Runners were disbanded in 1839; and when the Bow Street Police Office itself was moved in 1881, virtually all the official records of the men and their inaugural battle against crime were destroyed. The reason for this discarding of priceless information about the forerunners of a force that now prides itself on the care with which it treats all data and records is heart-breakingly simple. The documents were just not thought worth keeping. Certainly there are a few records about the Bow Street Runners to be found at Scotland Yard and in the Public Record Office; but all the day-to-day journals and lists of successful pursuits and prosecutions have long since gone. To some criminologists this has made the Runners seem more like characters from fiction than fact. But a real force they most definitely were. And according to a tribute in the *Daily Courant,* Sir Richard Blunt was 'one of the most acute, active and personally daring of the magistrates of London'. A man known for the zeal with which he pursued all law-breakers.

Sir Richard came from a wealthy London banking family of Essex Street, a small turning to the left at the top of Fleet Street where it joins The Strand. He was a man who evidently believed strongly in the ideals of Henry Fielding and the Bow Street Runners and had been most happy to be recruited to their ranks. As a person of considerable private

means, he had the time as well as the inclination to devote himself to
detective work whenever a case worthy of his mettle arose. It seems
highly likely that Blunt himself felt there must be more to the stories of
a 'horrid smell' emanating from St Dunstan's Church than was first
apparent. Reports about this had been brought to him by Mr Otton,
the Beadle of St Dunstan's, who also served as the parish constable. An
account which subsequently appeared in the *Daily Courant* explains
how the whole curious business began:

'The matter came to light when the pious pages of the frequenters
of St Dunstan's Church began to perceive a strange and most
abominable odour throughout that sacred edifice. It was in vain that
old women who came to hear the sermons, although they were too
deaf to catch a third part of them, brought smelling-bottles and other
means of stifling their noses. Notwithstanding this, still the dreadful
charnel-house sort of smell would make itself most painfully and
disagreeably apparent.'

It was not long, says the *Daily Courant* before complaints were
being made to the priest at St Dunstan's. In this and one or two other
early accounts of the Sweeney Todd story, the clergyman is named as
the Reverend Joseph Stillingport. However, research by Maureen
Shillingford Schlegal of Philadelphia, into the legend of the demon
barber in connection with her own family name indicates that the
correct spelling of the reverend gentleman's name was Shillingford
who, records she has found for this date, list as the priest in charge at
St Dunstan's Church. Contemporary reports are, however, agreed that
the poor man was regularly upset by the terrible smell and made to
sneeze during his sermons, 'and to hold to his pious mouth a
handkerchief, in which was some strong and pungent essence, for the
purpose of trying to overcome the horrible effluvia.' The *Daily
Courant* continues its report:

'The organ-blower and the organ-player were also both nearly
stiffled, for the offensive odour seemed to ascend to the upper part of
the church, although those who sat in what may be called the pit by
no means escaped it. The churchwardens also wore contorted
countenances and were almost afraid to breathe.

'The only person who did not complain bitterly of the dreadful
odour in St Dunstan's Church was an old woman who had been a
pew-opener for many years. But it was said she had lost the facilities of

her nose, which probably accounted for the circumstance.

'As might be supposed, from the fact that this sort of thing had gone on for a few months, it began to excite some attention with a view to a remedy. For in the great city of London a nuisance of any sort or description requires to become venerable by age before anyone thinks of removing it. The church-wardens also began to fear that some pestilential disease would be the result if they for any longer period of time put up with the horrible stench, and so began to institute enquiries about what could be done to obviate it.'

Constable Otton, in the best tradition of the Bow Street Runners, reported the matter to his chief. What puzzled him, he said, was that the smell reminded him of putrefying corpses; yet no one had been buried in the church for many years.

Richard Blunt's first action was to pay a visit to St Dunstan's with Constable Otton. There, armed with cloths soaked in vinegar for their noses, he and the constable explored both the main body of the church and the vaults below. The stench was certainly overpowering; but no matter where they looked, no immediate cause could be found. There were no signs of any vaults having been opened or any of the notorious sewers in the vicinity having burst. Sir Richard and his man left the church none the wiser.

Just when it seemed the source of the problem of the stench-ridden church might prove insoluble, a crucial piece of gossip from the same neighbourhood reached the magistrate. Again it was passed on by one of his constables and, although initially there was no suggestion the two events might be linked, it certainly opened up a new line of enquiry. The story concerned the barber at 186 Fleet Street – a man called Sweeney Todd. Apparently, according to local gossip, a number of customers, including several sea-faring men, had used the shop and then had never again been seen. Sir Richard had never been a man to jump to conclusions, but his instincts told him he might just be onto something.

Of course, in a sprawling metropolis like London, the coming and going of people was never easy to keep track of – certainly not that of seamen who were in and out of the port all the time. But the stories had a persistence about them; and there was something familiar to Sir Richard about the name Sweeney Todd – it was one of those unusual names that stuck in the mind.

Sir Richard, the evidence suggests, consulted the records of the Bow

Street Runners, and there found that Todd had actually appeared before him in court. Although there is only one brief reference to this incident in a fictionalised version of Sweeney Todd's life, it has the ring of truth about it. It suggests an excellent reason why Blunt decided to initiate investigations into the barber, leading him eventually to link the events in Todd's shop with those in the church. The story is told in *Sweeney Todd* by James McDonald (1910):

'Some years earlier, a lady walking along Fleet Street was attracted by a pair of shoe-buckles, studded with imitation diamonds, which were being worn by Sweeney Todd. She screamed out and declared that they belonged to her husband, who had gone out one morning from his house in Fetter Lane to be shaved, but had never returned.

'After the lady had established the identity of Todd she instituted proceedings which came before Sir Richard Blunt. However, the buckles were of too common a kind for the lady to persevere in her statement, and Todd, who maintained the most imperturbable coolness throughout the affair, was, of course, discharged.

'The matter did though leave a suspicion in the magistrate's mind. Other affairs, however, of more immediate urgency occupied his time, but the report by the constable of the stories regarding Todd revived ail his former feelings and made him believe sharp and prompt attention was called for.'

Despite the fact that there is no documentation to support this story, circumstantial evidence lends weight to it being possible. In any event, Sir Richard Blunt now ordered his men to keep a watch on Sweeney Todd's shop while he himself reported his suspicions to the Secretary of State. Following a meeting with the government minister, he was given permission to continue the surveillance of Todd and 'use what means might be necessary' to get to the bottom of the mystery.

The decision to post the Runners in premises opposite 186 Fleet Street paid dividends for Sir Richard when, in the ensuing months, reports reached his office of at least three customers entering the shop who had not been seen to leave. He ordered his men to enter the barber's shop with as many clients as possible to keep an eye on them. To hasten his inquiries before more lives were lost, Blunt decided to search the vaults of St Dunstan's once again, accompanied by a party of Bow Street Runners. He was growing ever more convinced that if

Sweeney Todd *was* killing his customers and hiding the bodies, it had to be somewhere in the adjoining cellars of the church. What he found on this new expedition, however, opened up a new, totally unexpected and gruesome element to the unfolding drama.

In his search of the vaults, Sir Richard made use of a special walking stick he had had made some years before. Underneath its gold top, the stick concealed a small compass; and the magistrate made use of this in order to explore the maze of corridors and passageways which he and his men had been nervous about entering on their previous visit. With only the lights of their oil lamps to aid them, the little party stumbled upon the grave of the Weston family and its grisly remains of human bodies. Going further, following the unmistakable tracks of human footsteps in the dirt and rubble, the Runners suddenly found themselves at the back to Mrs Lovett's underground cookhouse. The bloodstained evidence which Sir Richard Blunt saw there confirmed a nightmare he had been reluctant to admit to himself: Sweeney Todd was not only a mass murderer, but he was getting rid of the evidence by turning it into meat pies.

The minds of the men who trudged back along those passageways to the church must have been full of a mixture of revulsion and horror. They were determined to bring to justice the man who could perpetrate such evil – and his partner, too.

The readings from his compass enabled the magistrate to decide without much difficulty that the shop of Sweeney Todd's accomplice was in Bell Yard. Two Runners were at once despatched to keep watch on these premises, too. Before the day was out, Sir Richard Blunt had on his desk a memorandum about Mrs Lovett and what details were known of her.

Although the magistrate was now satisfied in his own mind about the collusion between the barber and the pie-maker, he was still anxious for more specific evidence against Todd. The monster might have found an easy way of disposing of the bodies; but what was he doing with his victim's clothes and valuables? Sir Richard decided to send one of his men to search Sweeney Todd's premises. Several days passed before a suitable opportunity arose – but the wait was worth every minute. The Runner who gained access to the building found several cupboards full of clothing and a drawer packed with valuables. Taking details of the names and initials on some of the hats and gold watches, he hurried back with the information to Craven Street.

Sir Richard now acted quickly. Three of his most senior constables were sent off to Bell Yard with a warrant for Mrs Lovett's arrest. He and the remaining men set out for Fleet Street.

Some of the more colourful accounts of the story of the Demon Barber claim that when Mrs Lovett was arrested in her shop as she was serving a group of customers, such was the outcry that she had to be saved from being lynched.

'The people who were in the shop spread the news all over the neighbourhood,' says the Charles Fox version, 'and the place was soon jammed up with a maddened mob. They poured in from Fleet Street and Carey Street determined to tear her to bits and hang her on the lamp post in the middle of Bell Yard.' The Bow Street Runners, however, as good as their name, were able to spirit Mrs Lovett out of the back of the house into a waiting coach and driver her speedily to Newgate.

The vivacious young widow was a shadow of her former self by the time she reached the great, grey prison. Her face was white and drawn, her eyes wild with fear. All her beauty and composure had drained away. To the men who sat silently on each side of her, she blurted out her confession. Sweeney Todd had been the murderer – she was just his accomplice. The Demon Barber was the man they should arrest. Neither man spoke a word of reply or comfort during the journey. Once inside the prison Mrs Lovett, her nerve gone, demanded to see the Governor. She wanted to make a statement, she said, she was not going to be blamed for everything.

A version of Mrs Lovett's confession, printed by the *London Chronicle*, is probably accurate in essence, although it does offer a slightly different version of certain elements in the story.

'Believing that I am on the edge of the grave, I, Margery Lovett make this statement.

'Sweeney Todd first conceived the idea of that mutual guilt which we have both since carried out. He bought the house in Bell Yard, as likewise in Fleet Street, and by his own exertions he excavated an underground connection between the two, mining right under St Dunstan's Church, and through the vault of that building.

'When he had completed all his arrangements he came to me and made his offer. But he did not tell me that these arrangements were then complete as that, he doubtless thought, would have placed him too much in my power in the event of my refusing to co-operate with him in his iniquity. He need not have given himself that amount of trouble – I was willing.

'The plan he proposed was that the pie-shop should be opened for the sole purpose of getting rid of the bodies of people whom he might think proper to murder in or under his shop. He said that, fearing nothing and believing nothing, he had come to the conclusion that money was the greatest thing to be desired in this world, inasmuch as to it he had found that all people bowed down.

'He said that after the murder of anyone, he would take the flesh from the bones quickly and convey it to the shelves of the bakehouse in Bell Yard, the pieces to be materials for the pies. Minor arrangements he left to me. He murdered many. The business went on and prospered and we both grew rich. This is how we fell to our present state.'

After she fell silent, Mrs Lovett was asked by the Governor of Newgate if she had anything further to add. Shaking her head, she only enquired if her confession would be used against Sweeney Todd as well as herself.

'Yes, it is strong corroboration of the evidence against him' she was told, 'and, as such, if there had been any doubt, would have gone far towards making his conviction certain.'

Unaware that he already had the most crucial evidence against Sweeney Todd, Sir Richard Blunt and his men strode into 186 Fleet Street to write the last chapter in the bloody saga of the Demon Barber.

12

The Trial of The Age

Investigating gruesome crimes in London was not altogether new to the Bow Street Runners, but the men who went with Sir Richard Blunt to Sweeney Todd's barber shop in Fleet Street in October 1801 must have wondered quite what kind of coldblooded killer they would find there: a man who could calmly cut up bodies and then see the remains made into meat pies for public consumption. Though some of the officers might have recalled a grisly case which had occurred earlier in the same year on 26 April. The event has been reported in the *Annual Register*.

'About 8 in the evening,' it began, 'a mob assembled before a house in Wych Street, formerly the Queen of Bohemia Tavern (but now supposed to be unoccupied), in consequence of some boys who had been at play in the passage declaring they saw some persons through the keyhole employed in cutting up human bodies. The mob having increased, at length broke into the house in which they found several human bodies partly dissected, one body of a man who appeared to have been not long dead, with that of an infant not four months old, untouched, and several tubs with human flesh, etc.

'The stench was so great that many were glad to return without viewing the disgusting scene, and many who went in were seized with sickness. Notwithstanding it was explained to the mob that the house had been for some time used as an anatomical theatre, they were so enraged as to proceed to destroy the house.

'But a party of Bow Street officers arriving, at length succeeded in restoring peace to the great satisfaction of the neighbourhood who had been much alarmed at the idea that the mob would in their rage set fire to the house. The surgeons who were in the house made their escape by a back way, leaving several of their instruments behind them.'

Nothing so dramatic happened when Sir Richard Blunt and his men burst in on Sweeney Todd. The group of officers apparently established that the barber was alone before entering the shop. The magistrate immediately instructed that the front door and passage to the rear were to be covered to prevent any possible escape. With the traditional Runners' cry of 'Clap the darbies on his wrists!' Sweeney Todd was seized and handcuffed before he could cry out or make a move. He stood, looking bewildered, as Sir Richard Blunt informed him he was being arrested for murder.

The available evidence suggests that Todd once again tried to brazen it out with the man he had confronted before in court. A claim in a colourful version of the legend that one of the Bow Street Runners suggested the Demon Barber should be fastened into his own revolving chair in order to extort a confession from him, may be dismissed as mere sensationalism. Another claim that he tried to break free of the arresting officers and threatened them with the razor hidden up his sleeve is as doubtful as a statement that he simply broke down and wept. All that is certain, however, is that Sweeney Todd was arrested and taken away by coach to Newgate. Unlike the arrest of Mrs Lovett, not a single member of the public knew about the seizure of the barber until he was safely behind bars.

The news of Mrs Lovett's confession must have sealed Sir Richard Blunt's delight that day. He had arrested a mass-murderer, probably the worst ever known in London, and he had the evidence of Todd's partner to help convict him. The magistrate left behind two of his officers at 186 Fleet Street with orders to comb every inch of the property and list each item they found. The pair were to have their work cut out during the new few days, so enormous did the task prove.

The news of Mrs Lovett's arrest had spread through London like wildfire. But the horror which had greeted the revelations about what had been going on in her shop was far surpassed on the following day by the announcement from the Bow Street Office in Craven Street that Sweeney Todd had been arrested for murder and suspected collusion with the pie-maker of Bell Yard.

London had never known such a sensation before. What little information the newspapers were supplied with before the trial was more than compensated for by public rumour, as an undated clipping from *The Examiner* of this time makes plain:

'By the time the police office at Bow Street had opened the following morning, a wild, vague and uncertain rumour had spread itself over London concerning the discoveries that had been made at Sweeney Todd's house in Fleet Street and Mrs Lovett's in Bell Yard, Temple Bar.

'The affair lost nothing from many tongued rumour and the popular belief was that Sweeney Todd's house had been found full of dead bodies from the attics to the cellars, while Mrs Lovett had been actually detected in the very act of scraping some dead man's bones for tit-bits to make a veal pie.

'Dense crowds assembled in Fleet Street to have a look at Todd's now shut-up house, and that thoroughfare, in consequence, very soon became no thoroughfare at all. Bell Yard, too, was so completely blocked up that the lawyers who were in the habit of using it as a short cut from the Temple to Lincoln's Inn were forced to take a diversion through Chancery Lane instead.

'In Bow Street, and round the doors of the police office there, was a dense crowd, too, anxious for news of the affair, and it was only with the greatest difficulty that the officers and others connected with the police inquiries could get in and out as occasion required.'

Interest in the case was to continue unabated in the weeks which followed, while Sir Richard Blunt busied himself preparing the evidence for the trial. He was to wish things could have moved faster when, a few days before Christmas, he received a crashing piece of information from Newgate. Mrs Lovett had somehow managed to get hold of some poison and had been found dead in her cell.

The details have never been quite clear as to just how the widow managed to obtain the poison with which she committed suicide. Probably because she was a woman of means she was able to pay one of the guards to have some clean clothes from home brought in to her; and it is possible there was a vial of poison concealed in one of the dresses in readiness for such an eventuality.

In any event, her body was discovered at about eight o'clock one morning just before Christmas. And with her death the prosecution lost one of their best witnesses against Sweeney Todd, for she had, since her arrest, once again confirmed to Sir Richard Blunt that she was prepared to turn King's Evidence. Now there would be no answer to perhaps the most intriguing question of all: *why* did she agree to help Sweeney

Todd in concealing his monstrous crimes? In her confession she said nothing beyond being his 'willing' accomplice. But was she willing because of her love for Todd? Or because she was afraid of him?

The news of Mrs Lovett's death dismayed Sir Richard Blunt who immediately ordered an inquiry into what had occurred. He also gave instructions that Sweeney Todd was not to be told about her death and the guard on him was to be redoubled. He did not want to lose the barber, too, especially with his trial only days away.

Christmas in London that year of 1801 was almost completely overshadowed by the coming trial of the 'Demon Barber of Fleet Street', as he had become known in the public prints. A leading article in the *Daily Courant* stated:

'Scarcely ever in London has such an amount of public excitement been produced by any criminal proceedings as by the trial of Sweeney Todd. The most hideous crimes have been laid to his charge, and, in the imagination of the people, the number of his victims has been quadrupled.

'So great is the excitement that sober-minded men, who do not see any peculiar interest in the sayings and doings of a great criminal, are disgusted that the popular taste should run that way. Be that as it may, the case of Rex v. Sweeney Todd will certainly be one of the trials of the age.'

And so it proved to be, as the account later prepared by *The Newgate Calendar,* from which I propose to quote at length, indicates. Such were the numbers of people trying to get into the Old Bailey for the trial, it says, that extra guards had to be placed in the court. The prisoner himself was brought from Newgate in irons which secured his ankles and wrists together and only enabled him to shuffle forward a few inches at a time.

It was only just before his departure for the court that Todd had been told of the death of Mrs Lovett. He looked, thereafter, the report says, 'like some great, gaunt ghost'. The haranguing he received from the sea of faces on all sides as he was lead into the court for the proceedings to begin could not have helped his complexion, either.

Once order had been restored in the packed Old Bailey, the judge and jury were told that the prisoner was charged with the murder of one Francis Thornhill, and he had originally been indicted with a female named Lovett. She, though, had taken her own life while in custody. The Attorney-General, who was presenting the prosecution's case, then began his address.

'The prisoner at the bar has been in business as a barber in Fleet Street for some years,' he said. 'Where he has continued to reside until his arrest upon the serious charge which we are brought here to investigate. What were the pursuits of the prisoner during his occupancy of that house, it is not our province just now to enquire, as all our attention must be directed to the consideration of the one charge, to which he stands at the bar of this court.'

The lawyer then began to outline the evidence that Sir Richard Blunt and his men had so painstakingly gathered from their investigations into the contents of Sweeney Todd's shop and the vaults of St Dunstan's Church.

'It appears that upon the third day of August last, a ship of 400 tons burthen, called *The Star,* arrived in the London Docks. On board that ship was the captain, a crew of nine seamen, and two boys. As passengers there were a Colonel Jeffrey and the Mr Thornhill whose death is the motive of these preceedings.

'Now this Mr Thornhill had been commissioned to take a certain string of Oriental pearls, valued at about £16,000, to a young lady in London. He was anxious to fulfil this request, and as soon as the ship docked went into the City with the pearls. It appears that upon his route to deliver them, he went into the shop of the prisoner at the bar to be shaved, and no one ever saw him come out again.'

The Attorney-General hitched his gown around his shoulders and went on without a pause: 'My Lord and gentlemen of the jury, when Mr Thornhill did not return, the captain of the ship and Colonel Jeffrey became very anxious about him and made every inquiry as to his whereabouts. They questioned the prisoner at the bar, who admitted that he had shaved Mr Thornhill, but he had left the shop when the operation was over.

'When *The Star* and her captain were forced to leave London for Bristol,' the Attorney General continued, 'Colonel Jeffrey decided to remain in the City to continue his inquiries as he felt sure that such a valuable string of pearls was bound to turn up again.

'Gentlemen, it did,' he said. 'It appeared at the Hammersmith residence of Mr John Mundel who lent money upon securities, and it will be deposed that one evening the prisoner at the bar went to this

Mr Mundell and pawned a string of pearls for £1,000. It is to be regretted that this Mundell cannot be brought before the jury for he is dead. But a confidential clerk, who saw the prisoner at the bar, will depose the facts.' The Attorney General paused. 'These facts,' he went on, 'connect' the prisoner with the disappearance of Thornhill – but now we come to the strongest features of this remarkable case. It appears that for a considerable time the Church of St Dunstan's in Fleet Street had become insufferable from a peculiar stench which seemed to fill the entire edifice, and quite baffled the authorities.'

The Attorney General explained to the court that no one had thought to thoroughly examine the vaults until Sir Richard Blunt, the police-magistrate, had undertaken the task. 'Gentlemen of the jury,' he said, 'Sir Richard found that almost every vault was full of the fresh remains of the dead. He found that into old coffins, the tenants of which had mouldered to dust, there had been thrust fresh bodies, with scarcely any flesh remaining on them – but yet sufficient to produce the stench in the church. One vault was found, the contents of which are too horrid to describe, but suffice to say that it contained what butchers when speaking of slaughtered animals call "offal".'

Even the hardened people of London well used to hearing ghastly tales of atrocities fell silent at this. All their eyes were on the Attorney-General as he continued with his remarks:

'Well, my Lord and gentlemen of the jury, Sir Richard persevered in his investigations and found that there was an underground connection from beneath the shaving shop of the prisoner, and the cellarage of a house in Bell Yard, Temple Bar, which was occupied by a female named Lovett, who this day should have stood at the bar beside the prisoner had she not, despite every vigilance used to prevent such an act, succeeded in poisoning herself while in prison in Newgate.

'It will be shown in evidence that the way the larger portion of the flesh of Sweeney Todd's victims was got rid of was by converting it into meat and pork-pies on the premises of Mrs Lovett.'

Even though what the prosecuting counsel had said was common gossip around London, his words still drew an audible gasp from the packed public benches. When silence had fallen once again, the Attorney-General went on to describe Sweeney Todd's revolving chair in which he had killed his victims or left them so stunned that he could easily cut their throats.

'And now, my Lord, and you gentlemen of the jury, may ask what these wholesale murders have to do with the indictment which simply charges the prisoner with the wilful murder of Francis Thornhill? To this I reply that it is impossible to make apparent to the court the method by which Francis Thornhill came to his death without going into these painful details.'

The Attorney-General paused once more and then delivered a second bombshell into the quiet of the packed Old Bailey courtroom.

'Sweeney Todd's house was found crammed with property and clothing sufficient for *160 people.*'

For a moment there was a stunned silence. Men and women looked at each other in disbelief. Had they heard right? The rumours had suggested he might have cut the throats of *dozens* of victims. But *over a hundred.* Could it possibly be true?

'Yes, gentlemen of the jury,' the barrister spoke with heavy emphasis in his voice as if to dispel any doubts, 'I said 160 people, and among all that clothing was found a piece of jacket which will be sworn to have belonged to Francis Thornhill.'

In repeating that number, *The Newgate Calendar* reported, the counsel released 'a thrill of horror' into the court, and it was to be some moments before order could be restored and the proceedings continue.

'But, my Lord, is a piece of sleeve enough to convict a man? Wisely, the law says no and looks for the body of a murdered man. Indeed, I do not call to mind an instance of a conviction where there has not been some satisfactory identification of the remains of the murdered man. We will produce that proof.

'For among the skeletons found contiguous to Todd's premises was one which will be sworn to as being that of the deceased Mr Thornhill. One bone of that skeleton will be produced in court and sworn to by a surgeon, Doctor Steers, who had the care of it and who, from repeated examinations such as only he could make, knows it well. That, my Lord and gentlemen of the jury, is all I have to say for the prosecution.'

As the Attorney-General sat down, all eyes in the courtroom turned upon Sweeney Todd. He had sat impassively throughout the address and still nothing seemed to disturb his features even now.

The first witness was Arthur Rose Ford, the captain of *The Star,* who confirmed that Francis Thornhill had sailed on his ship, been in possession of a string of valuable pearls, and had never been seen again after his visit to Sweeney Todd's shop. Into the witness box after him came Colonel William Jeffrey who also gave his account of the disappearance of Francis Thornhill, and how he had gone to Sir Richard Blunt to ask for his help.

'I accompanied Sir Richard and Doctor Steers to Sweeney Todd's shop,' the Colonel said, 'and in the vaults below, saw the Doctor take a bone from there. I made a mark on the bone to ensure its identification.'

The smartly dressed military man had hardly stepped down from the witness box, than his place was filled by the tall and impressive figure of Sir Richard Blunt. His was the evidence that all London had been waiting to hear. This was the Bow Street Runner who had run the cut-throat killer to ground. For the first time, too, Sweeney Todd was observed to look up at the man in the box. He was even noticed to cup a hand to one of his ears as if to hear better.

The police-magistrate was asked by the Attorney-General to relate in his own words his part in the events now before the court. In a quiet and precise voice, Sir Richard started by explaining how his attention had been drawn to the number of people who had unaccountably disappeared in the vicinity of Fleet Street.

'Not a trace could be found of many respectable men who had left their homes upon various objects and never returned to them,' Sir Richard said. 'The most striking peculiarity of this affair was that the men who disappeared were for the most part substantial citizens who were far from likely to have yielded to any of those temptations that at times bring the young and heedless in this city into fearful dangers. I saw the Secretary of State upon the matter and it was agreed that I was to have *carte blanche* to give my time and attention to unravelling the mystery.

'After careful inquiry, I found that out of thirteen disappearances, no less than ten had declared their intention to get shaved, or their hair dressed, or to go through some process which required them to visit a barber. I then personally called at all the barbers' shops in the neighbourhood – but never alone.

'The fact that I had someone waiting for me in the shop doubtless saved my life – for *I* was several times shaved and dressed by the prisoner at the bar.'

Sir Richard's words resounded in the stillness of the Old Bailey with all the impact of the earlier surprises which the case had produced. One legend suggests that Sweeney Todd himself sat bolt upright in his chair at this confession by the Bow Street Runner. The very man who was now the main witness against him could so easily have been numbered among his victims.

The magistrate admitted to the court that he had found nothing suspicious on any of these visits, though he remembered that on a couple of occasions the barber had attempted to get Sir Richard's companion to leave the shop on some pretext. When the man had refused to go, Sweeney Todd had 'gone on with the shaving in the coolest possible manner'.

The breakthrough in his investigations had come with the reports of the strange smell at St Dunstan's, Sir Richard told the court.

'My attention was directed to the peculiar odour in the church and from that moment I, in my own mind, connected it with Sweeney Todd and the disappearances of the persons who had so unaccountably been lost in the immediate neighbourhood of Fleet Street. And in the midst of this, I had a formal application made to me concerning the disappearance of Mr Francis Thornhill, who had been clearly traced to the shop of the prisoner at the bar and never seen by anyone to leave it.'

Convinced, now, that the solution to the mystery lay in or below Sweeney Todd's shop, the magistrate said he had instituted a thorough search unknown to the owner.

'In the cellar beneath the shop, the first object that presented itself to me was a chair fixed to the roof by its legs. The chair I at once recognised as identical to the one in the shop on which I had sat. In a moment the whole truth burst upon me.'

Following his discovery of this chair which precipitated the unsuspecting victims into the cellar, Sir Richard said he next found some bodies hidden in the vaults and then the passageway to Mrs Lovett's pie shop in Bell Yard.

'Prosecuting my researches, I also found that no meat from any butcher or salesman ever found its way to the pie shop,' he continued. 'The supply of flesh was human and that was the way the prisoner had got rid of the greater part of his victims.

'Measures were then taken to prevent any more murders by persons in my force always following anyone into the barber's shop. Then, when the evidence was all ready by the finding and identifying of Mr Francis Thornhill's leg-bone, I took measures to apprehend the prisoner.'

One final witness for the prosecution then entered the box, Doctor Sylvester Steers, the specialist who had identified the leg bone of the murder victim.

The Doctor told the court of his visit to the vaults of St Dunstan's Church.

'I found there a great quantity of osteological remains, human bones,' he said, 'and among them a male femur, or thigh bone, which I have with me.'

As Doctor Steers spoke, *The Newgate Calendar* reports, he took from the pocket of his great-coat, a small packet wrapped in brown paper. Untying some string, he extracted a small bone and handed it to a court official. 'It was passed to the jury,' says the report, 'but several shrank from it.'

The Attorney-General addressed the witness: 'Can you, sir, on your oath and without the slightest reservation, tell my Lord and the gentlemen of the jury, whose thigh bone this is?'

'I can. It is the thigh bone of Mr Francis Thornhill'

'Will you tell the court the grounds upon which you arrived at that conclusion?'

'Certainly. Mr Thornhill met with a very unusual and painful accident. The external condyle or projection on the outer end of the thigh bone, which makes part of the knee-joint, was broken off, and there was a diagonal fracture about three inches higher up upon the bone. I had the sole care of the case, and although a cure was effected, it was not without considerable distortion of the bone and general disarrangement of the adjacent parts.'

Doctor Steers added, 'From my frequent examination I was perfectly well acquainted with the case, and I can swear that the bone in the hands of the jury was the one so broken and to which I attended.'

The Attorney-General had one final question for the witness. 'Did you ever have a similar case to that of Mr Thornhill's under your treatment?'

'No, sir. Never a precisely similar one.'

As the Doctor climbed down from the witness box and returned to his seat, the bone which he had brought as evidence was retrieved by the court official from the last of the jurors and placed carefully on the table in front of the legal counsels. There was undeniably something both eloquent and unnerving about that mute object which, for a moment in time, held the attention of every person in the packed courtroom of the Old Bailey. Could something so insignificant from such an overwhelming horror finally bring the terrible Demon Barber of Fleet Street to justice?

13

'Foul and Unnatural Murder'

The Newgate Calendar, in describing the trial of Sweeney Todd, states that it was 'quite clear to even the most superficial observer that the murder of Francis Thornhill had been just picked out for convenience sake, and was one among many'. When the counsel who had been appointed to represent the barber stood up to begin his defence, it was also soon apparent he was bent upon ridiculing the evidence that had been presented concerning the human bone which lay on the table in front of him.

'May it please your Lordship and gentlemen of the jury,' he began, 'I have, upon the part of my client, most seriously to complain about the vast amount of extraneous matter that has been mixed up with this case. To one grain of wheat we have had whole bunches of chaff, and gentlemen have been brought here surely to amuse the court with long-winded romances.

'My client is clearly and distinctly charged with the murder of one Francis Thornhill, and, instead of any evidence, near or remote fixing the deed upon him, we have nothing but long stories about vaults, bad odours in churches, movable floorboards, chairs standing on their heads, secret passages and pork pies. Really, gentlemen of the jury, I do think that the manner in which the prosecution has been got up against my virtuous and pious client is an outrage to your common sense.'

On hearing these words, an undercurrent of laughter arose from the public benches and the judge banged his gavel sharply several times to restore order. The defending counsel continued, totally unperturbed.

'This is nothing but the attempt to take the life of a man from a variety of circumstances external to the real charge to which he is called upon here to plead. Let us examine the sort of evidence upon which it had been thought proper to put a fellow creature to this bar upon a charge affecting his life.'

The speaker was clearly warming to his task and wondered, first, what the fact that a number of respectable men leaving their homes and never returning had to do with the death of Francis Thornhill?

'Then we are told that the respectable men want to get shaved,' he said. 'And that Sir Richard Blunt had a shave several times at my client's shop, yet here he is quite alive and well to give evidence today, and no one will say that Sir Richard is not a respectable man.'

The barrister paused as if to let his words sink in. He shuffled the sheaves of paper on the table in front of him before going on.

'Next we have the bad smell in the Church of St Dunstan. Really, gentlemen of the jury, you might well say that my client committed felony because this court was not well ventilated!'

For the second time that morning, a little wave of laughter broke the stillness of the Old Bailey. When it had subsided, defence counsel returned to his attack on the assumption that because Francis Thornhill had not been seen to come out of Sweeney Todd's shop he must have been murdered there.

'Really,' the barrister protested, 'this is too bad. Hundreds of people may have seen him come out – and no doubt did so – but they happened not to know him. So just because no one passed the time of day with this man, my client is declared guilty of murder.'

Pausing once again, the lawyer lent forward and lifted up the piece of bone from the table in front of him.

'Then we are told about this bone, and that it is declared to be the bone of the deceased. Gentlemen of the jury, what would you think of a man who should produce a brick and swear that it belonged to a certain house?

'I do think that you will soon see upon what a string of sophistry the evidence against my client rests. Who shall take it upon himself to say that Mr Thornhill is not alive and well somewhere? We all know that persons connected with the sea are rather uncertain in their movements.'

Shuffling his papers once again, the defence lawyer then turned on his heels to indicate the prisoner in the dock.

'My client, your Lordship and gentlemen of the jury, has a plain, unvarnished tale to tell which will clear him from any suspicions,' he said. 'Mr Todd is a religious man, as anyone may see by the mild and gentlemanly look of his amiable countenance. He took the premises in

Fleet Street in the pursuit of his most useful calling and he had no more idea that there was a movable floor in his shop, and that his shaving chair would go down with anyone, than an unborn child.

'Is it really likely that a man who could stoop to such baseness as to make money by murder would occupy himself with such a trivial employment as shaving for a penny? The deceased gentleman, Mr Francis Thornhill – if he be deceased at all – came into my worthy client's shop to be shaved, and was at that time a little the worse for drink that he had indulged himself with, no doubt, as he came along.

'My client did indeed shave him and he said that he had to go along and see a young lady. When he was shaved, Mr Thornhill left and went towards Fleet market. My client watched him from his door and actually saw him get into an argument with a porter at the top of the market. Then as another person came in to be shaved, my client returned into his shop and saw no more of Mr Thornhill.'

Referring to Todd as a 'man well-known for his benevolence and piety in Fleet Street', the barrister said that even during the time when the appalling smell at St Dunstan's was keeping many parishioners away, he faithfully attended the services: 'I ask you as men, my Lord and gentlemen of the jury, if you could do that in the knowledge that you had committed a murder?'

In his closing remarks, the defence counsel turned to the story of Mrs Lovett.

'My Lord, it is for my client a most unfortunate thing that a person named Lovett, who kept a pie shop in Bell Yard, is not now in the land of the living. If she were so, there is no doubt that she would have told some true tale of how the vaults beneath the old church connected with her shop, and so cleared the prisoner at the bar of all participation in her crimes.

'That murder has been committed in conjunction with that woman, who committed suicide, rather than come forward and clear my client, against whom she had a spite, there can be no doubt.

'Gentlemen of the jury, it is the wrong man who now stands at the bar. The real murderer has yet to be discovered. I therefore call upon you in the name of justice to acquit my client.'

There can be little doubt that this lawyer faced with the unenviable task of defending Sweeney Todd gave a bravura performance, if a little theatrical and overstated. When asked by the judge if he proposed to call any witnesses, the defence counsel replied, 'No, no. Innocence is its own best safeguard.'

According to *The Newgate Calendar,* the Attorney-General then waived his right of reply. The judge's summing up was brief and to the point.

'The sequence of evidence by which it is attempted to bring this crime home to the prisoner at the bar lies within a very small compass indeed,' he said, 'Firstly, there is the tracing of Francis Thornhill to the prisoner's shop and his disappearance from thence. Then there is the thigh bone sworn to be that of Francis Thornhill and certainly found in such contiguity to his premises as to warrant a belief that he placed it there. Gentlemen of the jury, the case is in your hands.'

According to most accounts, the jury debated for less than five minutes before delivering their verdict: 'Guilty.'

Pandemonium broke out among the spectators and it was some time before the judge could again restore order. Then, says *The Newgate Calendar,* 'All eyes were turned upon the most dastardly criminal of the age, Sweeney Todd, who stood in the dock glaring at the foreman of the jury.'

The sentencing of criminals in 1802 did not require the judge to withdraw first. He simply took up a black cap and placed it over his wig.

'Prisoner at the bar,' he said, 'you stand convicted after a most patient trial by an impartial jury of your fellow countrymen, and on the clearest evidence, of the foul and unnatural murder of Francis Thornhill. It was a cold-blooded, dastardly deed. You must therefore prepare to leave this world and make your peace in another.

'On me only rests the painful duty of passing the dread sentence of the law. Have you anything to say why that sentence, which is one of death, should not be passed upon you?'

Sweeney Todd's response to this invitation are, apparently, almost as many and varied as the subsequent versions of his life and crimes. It has been suggested he immediately pleaded insanity; that he claimed he was the victim of a conspiracy; and that if Mrs Lovett had been present she would have been able to prove his innocence. All that seems certain is that he shouted out, 'I am not guilty!'

Before passing sentence the judge addressed a few further remarks concerning Sweeney Todd's crimes which would certainly be considered inappropriate today – if not actually ruled inadmissable – but which undoubtedly helped cement the legend of the Demon Barber.

'Sweeney Todd,' he said, 'you have been convicted of the crime of murder, and certain circumstances which it would have been improper to produce before this court in the progress of your trial, lead irresistibly to the belief that your life for years past has been one frightful scene of murder. Not only the unhappy gentleman for whose murder you now stand here has suffered from your frightful practices, but many others.

'It will be a satisfaction, too, to the court and the jury to know that the woman named Lovett, who the prisoner said would and could prove his innocence had she been alive, made, shortly before her death, a full confession, wherein she inculpated you most fearfully.'

The judge paused, cleared his throat and added, 'It is now my painful duty to pass upon you the sentence of the law, which is that you be taken from here to a place of execution and hanged by the neck until dead. May Heaven have mercy upon you. You cannot expect that society can do otherwise than put out of life someone who, like yourself, has been a terror and a scourge.'

The judge stood up and the court rose with him. Before Todd could protest any further he was hurried out of the courtroom as fast as the iron shackles on his legs would allow, and back to Newgate.

* * *

The legend of the Demon Barber was reported for all to read in the following days and weeks in the pages of newspapers and pamphlets. A thriving trade was also done in a 'most exact likeness of Sweeney Todd the Murderer, drawn from life while he was on trial,' according to the hawkers who peddled them at three pence a copy. (A rare example which has survived is reproduced in this book.) The man who had made corpses into meat pies also quickly became a bogeyman for parents to use to frighten naughty children. Conversely, the barbers of London found themselves being looked at with suspicion for months after the trial, and the trade in meat pasties suffered disastrously, too.

Not surprisingly, a favourite topic of gossip in the streets and taverns of London concerned just how many victims Sweeney Todd might have dispatched. A gaoler in Newgate Prison who claimed to have had charge of Todd, said that the barber had awoken from a nightmare one morning and told him he had been haunted all night long by the faces of his victims, 'a sailor, a quaker, a hundred others'. Other than this rather circumstantial story, the truth is that Todd never himself disclosed any figure.

Although evidence of all the clothing found in Sweeney Todd's shop adds weight to the figure of 'over 160 victims' quoted in court, it was not until 1831 that more remains found in the vaults beneath St Dunstan's Church went some way towards confirming it. A group of workmen engaged on rebuilding the church, dug up several heaps of bones all along an underground passageway stretching from Fleet Street to Chancery Lane. This had apparently been the route taken by Todd on his journeys to Mrs Lovett's pie-shop, and the bones were believed to be those of earlier victims he had buried before resorting to using the vaults which Sir Richard Blunt had stumbled upon. Even this, however, may not have been the full total, for the evidence suggests his reign of terror extended for almost seventeen years, and that he may well, at the height of his crimes, have been 'polishing off' a victim every month. We shall never know.

It is true that after his execution the facts about Sweeney Todd rapidly became distorted. Indeed, in most subsequent accounts of his life it is maintained that he was hung at Tyburn, the favourite spot for dispatching highwaymen. This, however, is patently untrue. Although Tyburn, which stood on a spot now occupied by the famous London landmark, Marble Arch, had been the place of execution for criminals since the twelfth century, records clearly state that it ceased this function in 1783 after the completion of the new Newgate Prison.

'Thereafter,' says Peter Aykroyd in his study of *Evil London* (1973), 'all criminals convicted of capital crimes committed in the city of London or the County of Middlesex were hanged there. There were pertinent reasons for the transfer of the function. The processions to Tyburn had become an "obstacle to traffic and a hindrance to business". Also, residents in the Tyburn neighbourhood which had become fashionable not only disliked the mobs which assembled for the executions but also disapproved of the gallows being so close to their houses.'

So much, I am afraid, for all the colourful tales of Sweeney Todd being transported in an open cart through the city of London in front of huge, jeering crowds, to be strung up at Tyburn. To the readers of the first 'penny dreadfuls', a death in the tradition of the 'knights of the road' was doubtless much more in keeping with Todd's grisly reputation than an execution in front of the grey walls of Newgate Prison. Indeed, it is not difficult to understand how the authors of this cheap form of Literature found it much more satisfying to write, 'Those who found themselves unwitting cannibals through Sweeney Todd pelted him all the way to the gallows.'

What is a fact is that Sweeney Todd was taken from his cell in Newgate Prison at 8am on the morning of Tuesday, 25 January, 1802 and hung on a portable scaffold erected near the main gate in front of a crowd estimated at many thousands. He apparently 'died hard' on the gallows, but there is no record of any last minute confession or admission.

Thereafter, as was customary, Todd's body was taken down after hanging for an hour and removed to the Royal College of Surgeons in the Old Bailey for dissection. This fate was considered part of any sentence for murder. It seemed doubly appropriate, too, to all those who had followed the course of the Demon Barber's crimes, that he should end his days as a pile of flesh, bones and offal.

The greatest mass murderer in British history was just forty-six years old.

14

The Making of A Legend

The beginning of the Sweeney Todd legend in fiction and who was actually responsible for writing the first novelisation is surrounded by almost as much mystery, argument and conflicting claims as the life of the man himself. It has proved to be a tradition that has remained associated with the Demon Barber throughout the ensuing years. Whenever other writers have been attracted to the extraordinary saga of terror in the closing years of the Eighteenth Century – some of whose identities have also been open to dispute – each and every one has still played a part in helping to make Todd a source of continuing fascination: no matter how gruesome or unpleasant the facts may be.

It was not, in fact, until forty-five years after Sweeney's capture and execution at Newgate that his name appeared in print again. Curiously, it was to be in the pages of a rather sedately named weekly journal, *The People's Periodical and Family Library,* and not, as some authorities insist, a 'Penny Dreadful' of the type in which the bloody events in Fleet Street would be recycled ever more sensationally for subsequent generations of readers. There is, though, no question as to who was the publisher of this work, but its authorship may been the work of a single author or, possibly, that of a trio of writers. Investigating the facts concerning this publisher and his authors offers a fascinating insight into the early days of mass-market periodical publishing and the pressures put on those who wrote the stories for a demanding weekly readership.

For many years *The People's Periodical and Family Library* was regarded as an almost mythical publication. As recently as 1974 the historian, Michael Kilgarrif in his *Golden Age of Melodrama* wrote, 'This mysterious publication remains undiscovered.' Certainly copies of the periodical have long been incredibly rare – neither the British Museum nor the Bodlian Library possess any – and some writers have suggested that like the existence of the Demon Barber himself it, too, might be wholly fictitious. However, thanks to the renowned collector of 'Penny Dreadfuls,' David Philips, who managed to track down a complete run of *The People's Periodical and Family Library,* I was able to read the first dramatisation of the story of Sweeney Todd while I was researching this book and begin to understand how the legend had developed to its current enormous popularity. The story is certainly a seminal work in the history of the Demon Barber.

The People's Periodical was a sixteen-page paper about the same size as a modern women's magazine, illustrated with an engraving on the front page, and set in three columns of extremely small type. It featured mostly stories of romance with essays, reviews, answers to reader's letters and an 'Every-Day Book' of useful facts and figures. Material was obviously drawn from far and wide, and short stories by famous contemporary authors such as Charles Dickens and Edgar Allan Poe appeared frequently – doubtless reprinted without permission or payment because copyright protection of writers' work was then virtually non-existent. Although *The People's Periodical* serialised a few stories that enjoyed a certain popularity such as *Rose Somerville, Grace Weldon* and *The Fated Lovers of Bourdon,* it was the Sweeney Todd tale that has earned it a place in publishing history.

Todd made his bow in issue number seven of *The People's Periodical,* dated 21 November, 1846, as a character in a serial with the quite unremarkable title of *The String of Pearls: A Romance.* No author was credited for the story which began on the front page, although underneath the journal's masthead were the words, 'Edited by E. Lloyd'. Lloyd was also credited on the back page as being the printer and publisher, at his offices, 12 Salisbury Square, Fleet Street – a singularly appropriate address, I could not help thinking as I turned the fragile pages.

There was no hint, initially, that *The String of Pearls* was anything other than one of the magazine's usual pieces of romantic fiction; certainly nothing to suggest that it would feature real people and real events. Research has subsequently shown that this was an element frequently to be found in Lloyd's publications: he and his writers borrowed as freely from life as they did from fiction!

Although Sweeney Todd is introduced to the readers in the opening pages of the story, the half page engraving which accompanied the first episode depicted one of the most traditional situations in romantic literature – a pretty, tearful young girl, the heroine, Johanna Oakley, being comforted by her father. It was hardly the most dramatic introduction for a story that would run to thirty-seven chapters in eighteen subsequent issues, and help transform a sordid London murderer into a world-famous character.

Edward Lloyd (1815-1890) who described himself as the Editor of *The People's Periodical,* has subsequently become known as the founder of the 'Salisbury Square School of Fiction' – named after his address – and was certainly the most famous publisher of those weekly serials of the Victorian era known as 'Penny Bloods' or 'Penny Dreadfuls'. Although he made a fortune from these highly ephemeral publications, he later turned his back on such material and thereafter became a general newspaper publisher of – among other titles – *The Penny Sunday Times,* which later became *Lloyd's Weekly News* and survived well into the middle of the twentieth century as *The Sunday News.*

Lloyd was not only a very smart publisher, but also an unashamed self-publicist boasting in an issue of one of his papers: '*Lloyd's Weekly News* is the pioneer of cheap news for the people, as it is confessedly now the king of the weekly press. It is, and has ever been pre-eminent for priority of intelligence and the talent of its contributors, and its circulation far exceeds that of any contemporary.'

Lloyd, the son of a Thornton Heath farmer, was one of the pioneers of cheap literature for the masses in England. He took advantage of innovations in the printing industry, such as the development of the rotary steam printing press and the creation of paper-making machines, and the introduction of basic education for everyone, all of which were occurring at the onset of the nineteenth century, to do so. He himself had little formal education, but when he opened a small shop in London to sell books, newspapers and comic valentines, he quickly sensed a need for cheap, printed reading matter at a time when most literature was being published in expensive two and three volume books.

Working in London, Lloyd also became aware of the public's fascination with crime and criminals, and his very first publications in the late 1830s, sold for a penny and embellished with 'fierce' engravings, were full of such characters as their titles bear witness: *Lives of the Most Notorious Highwaymen, The History of Pirates* and *The Calendar of Horror* – an unashamed plagiarism of *The Newgate Calendar.*

The stories were scarcely works of literature. Most were churned out by poorly paid hacks who were encouraged to steal mercilessly from any sources and 'beef up' the material if the facts were not exciting or gruesome enough for a predominantly working-class market. Indeed, Lloyd and his successors often demonstrated their indifference to any finer feelings their readers might have by abruptly discontinuing episodes of the stories on one page of an issue, and then continuing in the next without even a word of 'what had gone before'!

With the benefit of hindsight, there can be little doubt that the engravings which adorned these 'penny dreadfuls' played an important part in their success, and it was by no means uncommon for a publication whose sales were flagging to have a sensational and even totally irrelevant picture inserted in an attempt to bolster public interest. If this had no effect, the whole story might well be brought to a speedy conclusion in the next issue without the least regard to the complexity of plot or variety of characters and the different situations in which they were involved.

In the twenty years between 1836 and 1856, Edward Lloyd published well over 200 such 'bloods' on almost every imaginable subject, but of all these, only two are remembered today: *The String of Pearls* which featured Sweeney Todd, and *Varney the Vampire,* a mammoth serial of 220 chapters about a marauding vampire in England which was published in penny parts in 1847. Both of these stories have been credited to a single member of Lloyd's team of writers, a remarkable man by the name of Thomas Peckett Prest (1810-1859) but this has been disputed as we shall see.

Prest is one of the most intriguing figures in the whole field of mass market literature. Historian W. O. G. Lofts, who has researched Prest's life, says that a very old man he spoke to some years back who had a personal knowledge of the writer described him as a 'morbid genius' who was regarded by his readers at the time as something of a second Edgar Allan Poe. However inflated such a claim may be, Mr Lofts is right in stating that Prest deserves better than to be totally ignored by all biographical dictionaries, for he was a writer of prodigious output and variety, and was certainly the most important of Lloyd's contributors. Despite the difficulty in attribution because of the lack of author credit on most of the Lloyd publications, Prest more than likely wrote over half of the 'penny bloods' originating from Salisbury Square.

According to the available evidence, Prest was born about 1810 into a comparatively affluent London family. He appears to have developed an absorbing passion for writing during his childhood – as well as a taste for languages, music and drama – and first ventured into print with some essays, articles and short stories contributed to weekly magazines in the 1830s. In November 1835 he took his first major step in journalism when he was appointed editor of *The Magazine of Curiosity and Wonder,* published by G. Drake of Clare Market, London, a publication packed with items about the strange and the mysterious. Despite its obvious appeal, the magazine only lasted for twenty-nine issues, but it undoubtedly furthered Prest's fascination with the bizarre.

His interest in music and the theatre saw him for a time act as editor of *The London Singer's Magazine,* as well as composing a number of music hall songs for popular artists of the day like George Leybourne, 'The Great Vance'. Prest continued to develop his connections with the stage, and he later adapted a number of farces and melodramas from the French. He was also for a time associated with the Britannia Theatre in Hoxton, and between 1841 and 1849 wrote several plays for the manager, Sam Lane. We shall be returning to this association later when discussing the history of Sweeney Todd in the theatre.

But undoubtedly the association which kept him busiest was the one with Edward Lloyd whom he met around 1840. By all accounts, Prest was already displaying some of the unstable elements in his character, drinking heavily and always in debt. Lloyd, who could offer him immediate payment on delivery of each episode of a serial, was just the sort of man the improvident Prest would be attracted to, and there are stories that at the peak of his production he was turning in episodes for as many as six serials per week. For this he would be paid ten shillings per episode. The fact he was so busy for Lloyd seems to dispel another story that he was unreliable – although there does not seem much doubt that he regularly changed his address to avoid his creditors.

It is no surprise to learn that the pressures of all this work, plus his heavy drinking, damaged Prest's health and he died at his home in George Street, Islington on 5 June, 1859 from phlebitis, a painful inflammation of the veins. He was just 49 years old and despite his incredible productivity for Edward Lloyd died penniless. Because of the sheer output and range of his work, Prest was credited with having written the original *The String of Pearls* – an attribution which was reinforced by several later historians of the 'Penny Dreadful,' notably Montague Summers in his *A Gothic Bibliography* which listed thousands of ephemeral novels and pamphlets. Summers does, though, make an interesting proviso:

'The opening chapters [of *The String of Pearls*] were written by George Macfarren (1788-1843) who was obliged to abandon the work owing to blindness, a complete rest of the eyes having been imperatively ordered before an operation for cataracts. The story was taken up and completed with great vigour by Thomas Peckett Prest.'

Summers's offers no source for his information about Mcfarren or the writer's motivation to write the story. Certainly, though, both he and Prest were very familiar with London where they lived and had already written serials about crime and criminals in the capital. Some doubt must exist about Macfarren's contribution as Summers has wrongly attributed a number of other tiles from this era – not the least of them being the famous vampire novel, *Varney, The Vampire; or, The Feast of Blood* published by Lloyd in 1847 which ran to 109 issues, 220 chapters and a total of 868 pages. The bibliographer calls it unequivocally, 'The esteemed masterpiece of Thomas Peckett Prest.'

However, subsequent investigation by a number of historians – including myself – has established beyond doubt through the records of Edward Lloyd's business and stylistic comparison, that *Varney* is the work of another of the publisher's writers, James Malcolm Rymer (1804-1882) whose stories appeared anonymously or under at least seven different pseudonyms. Interestingly, for a number of years his real name was thought to be another of Thomas Peckett Prest's pen names! While Rymer's output was every bit as prolific as his colleague, he managed his working hours and finances with much more skill and died a wealthy man. According to Louis James in *Fiction for the Working Man 1830-50* (1973), at the height of his abilities, Rymer was 'writing ten serials simultaneously and at his death his estate was £8,000.'

Born in the Scottish Highlands, Rymer trained as a civil engineer and surveyor and moved to London in the middle 1830s. Despite this trade, Rymer appears to have been captivated with the idea of being an author and when he met Lloyd at the Mechanics' Institute in London was easily persuaded by the astute publisher to write material for him. Shortly thereafter Rymer gave up engineering entirely and joined Lloyd as one of his editors. Determinedly though he strove to be a superior novelist, the young Scotsman realized that while he might excel in the field of lower-class literature, the achievements of those he admired, such as Leigh Hunt, were beyond him. So, grudgingly content with his lot, he gave the reading public a string of entertaining and successful 'Penny Dreadfuls' including perhaps the most popular of the "later" Gothic novels, *The Black Monk* (1844), *The Mystery in Scarlet* (1884, the novel which so delighted Robert Louis Stevenson), *The White Slave* (1844, a scathing attack on religious hypocrisy) and two of the most famous heroines in this area of fiction, *Ada, The Betrayed* (1845) and *Jane Brightwell* (1846). But it is the author of Llyod's "most ghoulish and goriest publication" (E. S. Turner) that Rymer is best remembered, *Varney the Vampire*.

Arguably the most famous penny-issue novel after the story of Sweeney Todd, *Varney, The Vampire* has similarly attracted it fair share of discussion about authorship. Thanks to the assertion of Summers, Prest was the favourite for many years. Then one of the most famous collectors of 'Penny Dreadfuls,' Barry Ono (1876-1941) argued on behalf of Rymer and was soon drawing other support. The clincher came when the late Frank Algar, another respected name in the field, obtained a collection of Rymer's books and papers in which he had listed his works for Lloyd. Amongst the hand-written titles was clearly stated, *Varney the Vampire; or, The Feast of Blood.*

In 2002, Helen R. Smith, an authority on anonymous Victorian cheap literature and author *of Penny Dreadfuls and Boys Adventures* (1998) based on the Barry Ono collection in the British Library, advocated James Malcolm Rymer as the real author of *The String of Pearls*. Writing in her pamphlet, *New Light on Sweeney Todd, Thomas Peckett Prest, James Malcolm Rymer and Elizabeth Caroline Grey* she examined the various sources believed to have inspired the Sweeney Todd story in French and English magazines as well as the works of the three authors. In Rymer's mammoth serial, *Newgate* (1847) – which Summers also attributed to Prest – she found his 'invention' of an offal cellar as the setting for the beginning of the story significant and also an advertisement in another of Lloyd's newspapers which seemed to point to him as the author of *The String of Pearls*. Her argument continued:

'Rymer's imagination is more powerful than Prest's and his later tales experiment successfully with new formats, like the story begun from near its ending, retracing the action before a powerful climax, as in *The Oath* (1846) and *The Secretary* (1848). The beginning of *The Oath*, also published as *Brentwood of Brentwood*, with the villain regaining consciousness screwed down in a coffin in the crypt of St Paul's Cathedral, is a fine example of his morbid power. The extension of *The String of Pearls* detailing Sweeney Todd's escape from Newgate Prison, is typical of Rymer's work.'

But doubt has already been cast on this conclusion. Dick Collins writing in his introduction to *The String of Pearls: The Original Tale of Sweeney Todd* (2005) argues:

'But from Smith's evidence alone, we cannot simply hand it over to Rymer. What Smith failed to note was the advertisement referred, unequivocally, not to the 1847 original, but the second, longer and inferior 1850 version. The 1847 version was always referred to as simply, *The String of Pearls: A Romance* and by no other title; the subtitle *A Sailor's Gift* refers to the 1850 version only. Given the similarity between the expansions to *Varney* and those to *The String of Pearls,* it is quite possible that a third (fourth?) hack was brought in to rework the book in 1850 and that this was Rymer, adding to the already composite work. Both text and advertisement support this theory. Her reascription to Rymer cannot be taken as fact.'

And there the matter rests – for the moment. The true attribution may never be known. Yet it is interesting to wonder whose idea it was to submerge the grisly Demon Barber in a love story – author or publisher? – other than, possibly, to spare the stomachs of the more delicate readers of *The People's Periodical and Family Library.* What I am sure of is that the author used *The Newgate Calendar* – which Lloyd had already, of course, earlier plagiarised – as his source of reference. To these facts, the anonymous scribe also added his imagination and some new characters.

What is, though, beyond argument, is that *The String of Pearls: A Romance* was to inspire the later plagiarisms and variations that have ensured Sweeney Todd's immortality – fascinated as we may be by him or loathing every brutal and bloody action he perpetrates.

* * *

The story of *The String of Pearls* is set in Fleet Street in the year 1785. The characterisation of Sweeney Todd that is provided is, however, rather less of a terrifying figure than pictured in the later 'Penny Dreadful' versions:

'The barber was a long, low-jointed, ill-put-together sort of fellow,' the first episode informed readers. 'He has an immense mouth, and such huge hands and feet that he was, in his way, quite a natural curiosity. What was more wonderful, considering his trade, was that there never was such a head of hair as Sweeney Todd's. It was a most terrific head of hair, and as the barber kept all his combs in it – some people said his scissors likewise – when he put his head out of the shop door to see what sort of weather it was, he might be mistaken for some Indian warrior with a very remarkable head-dress.'

Todd is also said to have a squint and 'a disagreeable kind of unmirthful laugh which came at all sorts of odd times and would sometimes make people start, especially when they were being shaved'.

In short, though, the author said, 'People thought him a careless enough, harmless fellow, with not much sense in him, and at times they almost considered he was a little cracked. But there were others, again, who shook their heads when they spoke of him, and while they could say nothing to his prejudice, except that they certainly considered he was odd. But for all that, he did a most thriving business; and was considered by his neighbours to be a very well-to-do sort of man, and decidedly, in city phraseology, "warm".'

As the story opens, Todd has just taken on a new apprentice, a timid lad named Tobias Ragg, whom he has warned against spying on him or drawing conclusions from anything he sees or hears in the shop. The punishment, the boy is told, will be to have his throat cut from ear to ear.

When the barber has finished talking to Tobias a customer with a dog enters the shop. Sweeney is obviously ill-at-ease with the animal, but sends Tobias off on an errand. He then busies himself shaving the man and, in conversation, learns that his customer has just returned from a voyage to India, carrying a gift of valuable pearls for Johanna Oakley, the daughter of a local spectacle-maker, from her sweetheart, Mark Ingestre. At the mention of the pearls, Todd asks to be excused for a moment.

'Sweeney Todd walked into the back parlour and closed the door,' The narrative continues. 'There was a strange sound suddenly

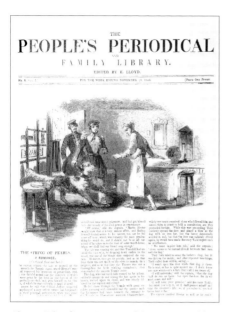

Below: George II, England's monarch during Sweeney Todd's time, cruelly nicknamed 'The Mad King'

Above: The first picture of Sweeney Todd in *The People's Periodical & Family Library,* November 8, 1846

Above: Lawless London: A 'Charlie' attacked by revellers. Late Eighteenth Century engraving by George Cruikshank

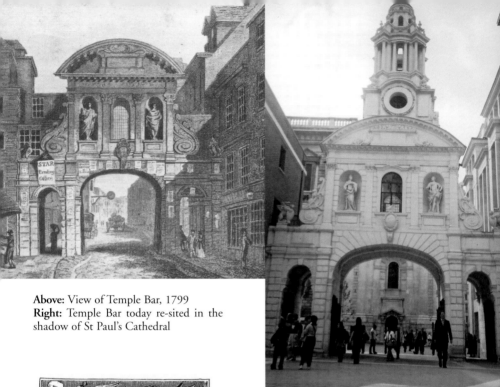

Above: View of Temple Bar, 1799
Right: Temple Bar today re-sited in the shadow of St Paul's Cathedral

Left: The heads of two traitors, Townley and Fletcher, provided a 'revolting spectacle' on Temple Bar during Sweeney Todd's era

Bottom Left: *Sweeney Todd, The Barber of Fleet Street* the first version of the story to carry the claim, 'Founded on Facts', circa 1881

Below: St Dunstan's Church in 1790 – Sweeney Todd's shop was located in the extreme right hand corner

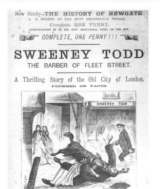

Above: St Dunstan's Church today – with the Law Courts in the distance

Right: Hen and Chicken Court which has changed little since the days of Sweeney Todd

Left: A classic engraving of the Demon Barber and his revolving chair, circa 1882

Right: Sweeney Todd was just one of the many London barbers who used the razors made by Henry Patten

Left: Vaults found beneath Fleet Street similar to those used by Sweeney Todd

Left: A romanticised engraving believed to be that of Mrs Lovett, the notorious pie maker

Bottom Left: An early Nineteenth Century engraving of Bell Yard where Mrs Lovett ran her pie shop

Bottom Right: The location of Mrs Lovett's pie shop is now adjacent to a surgery

Left: Mrs Salmon's Waxworks – one of the attractions of Fleet Street that enticed visitors to the area. Engraving by John Thomas Smith, 1793

Below: Bow Street where the hunt for the Demon Barber commenced. A contemporary engraving by George Cruikshank

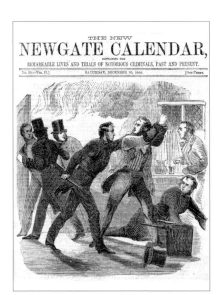

Left: The Newgate Calendar reported The Fleet Street Murders; in 1864

Below: Newgate Prison, shortly after it was rebuilt in 1780, where Sweeney Todd was held in custody

Left: Advertisement for the famous Charles Fox edition, *Sweeney Todd, The Demon Barber of Fleet Street*, published in 1878

Below: Famous melodrama villain, Mark Howard, starring in the Britannia Theatre production of Sweeney Todd, The Barber of Fleet Street, 1847

Above: An unusually mild-looking Sweeney Todd with his 'lather boy' in the American plagiarism *Sweeney Todd; or The Ruffian Barber* (1865)

Right: The murderous French barber, Barnabe Cabard in *The Inn of the Three Kings* by Jules Beaujoint (1890)

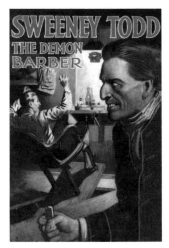
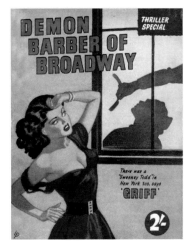

Above Left: The fascination with the Sweeney Todd legend never faltered in the Twentieth Century, with paperback versions of the story like this typical example, 1936

Above Right: *Demon Barber of Broadway* was by another author whose identity has been much debated since its publication in 1953

Left: Moore Marriott was the first actor to play the Demon Barber on the screen in *Sweeney Todd*, 1928

Left: Todd Slaughter, the archetypal Sweeney Todd on stage and screen for almost half a century, with Stella Rho as Mrs Lovett in the 1936 film

Left: Freddie Jones an excellent Sweeney Todd in the 1970 ABC TV version of the story for the series, *Mystery and Imagination*

Right: Denis Quilley and Shelia Hancock in the first London performance of Stephen Sondheim's musical, *Sweeney Todd* (1980)

Left: Ben Kingsley and Joanna Lumley in the Sky TV 1998 adaptation, *Sweeney Todd*

Right: A lip-smacking performance by Ray Winstone as the latest television Demon Barber in BBC TV's *Sweeney Todd*, broadcast in 2006

compounded of a rushing noise and then a heavy blow, immediately after which Sweeney Todd emerged from the parlour and, folding his arms, he looked upon the vacant chair where his customer had been seated. But the customer was gone, leaving not the slightest trace of his presence behind except for his hat, and that Sweeney Todd immediately seized and thrust into a corner of the shop.'

When the customer, a Lieutenant Thornhill, fails to return to his ship, two friends set out to find him. On the way they come across the man's dog, Hector, carrying a hat in his mouth. The animal leads them unerringly back to Sweeney Todd's shop. When the barber is confronted about the missing man, he admits he had shaved him, but the man had left without his hat. The dog had later rushed in behind another customer and ran off with it, he said. Neither of the men is satisfied with Sweeney Todd's story, but have no evidence to contradict him. When they leave the shop, the dog insists on remaining outside the door.

The story next introduces two more important female characters. The raven-haired, blue-eyed Johanna Oakley, who is awaiting the return of her lover, Mark: and the 'buxom, young and good-looking' Mrs Lovett who keeps a famous pie shop in Bell Yard. The shop is described in glowing terms:

'On the left-hand side of Bell-yard, going down from Carey-street, was, at the time we write of, one of the most celebrated shops for the sale of veal and pork pies that London ever produced. High and low, rich and poor, resorted to it; its fame had spread far and wide; and it was because the first batch of these pies came up at twelve o'clock that there was such a rush of the legal profession to obtain them.

'Well did they deserve their reputation, her famous pies,' the text continues. 'There was about them a flavour never surpassed and rarely equalled. The paste was of the most delicate construction and impregnated with the aroma of a delicious gravy that defied description. Then the small portions of meat which they contained were so tender, and the fat and lean so artistically mixed up, that to eat one of Mrs Lovett's pies was such a provocative to eat another, that many persons who came to lunch stayed to dine.'

But despite all these outward signs of a prospering business, Mrs Lovett is having trouble with her pie-maker who lives and works in the cellars beneath the premises and has announced he wants to leave the job. The place indeed seems far from an ideal working environment:

'It is a cellar of vast extent, and of dim and sepulchral aspect – some rough red tiles are laid upon the floor, and pieces of flint and large jagged stones have been hammered into the earthen walls to strengthen them; while here and there rough huge pillars made by beams of timber rise perpendicularly from the floor, and prop large flat pieces of wood against the ceiling to support it. Here and there gleaming lights seem to be peeping out from furnaces, and there is a strange, hissing, simmering sound going on, while the whole air is impregnated with a rich and savoury vapour.'

The pie-maker seems to have discovered something unpleasant about his work. But before he can carry out his threat, he is brutally murdered by an unseen assassin. Within a day, another poor wretch in need of work who calls himself Jarvis Williams calls at the shop and is offered the post of pie-maker.

Colonel Jeffrey, one of the missing Lieutenant Thornhill's friends, has now made himself known to Johanna Oakley and tells her about the seaman's disappearance on the way to see her with the string of pearls and a message from Mark. In company with another friend, Captain Rathbone, the Colonel has also spoken to Tobias Ragg and tried to get information from him about his master's activities. The boy is too frightened to talk – and with good reason. Tobias has, in fact, already discovered the secret of the barber's revolving chair and also found a number of cupboards full of items of clothing from previous customers. When Sweeney Todd realises the boy suspects him, he wastes no time in having Tobias committed to a disreputable madhouse.

At this juncture, Johanna Oakley has come to the conclusion that only by finding out what has happened to Thornhill can she hope to learn the fate of her lover. She takes the bold decision to disguise herself as a boy and seek a job as Sweeney Todd's apprentice. Her timing proves perfect with Tobias having just been committed, and she is given the job.

Colonel Jeffrey and Captain Rathbone have also not been inactive during the interim and have taken their suspicions about Sweeney Todd to 'a reknowned city magistrate', Sir Richard Brown. He, it seems, has already been investigating some strange reports of a horrid stench emanating from St Dunstan's Church and wonders if the two facts might in some way be connected:

'About this time, and while these incidents of our most strange and eventful narrative were taking place, the pious frequenters of old St Dunstan's Church began to perceive a strange and a most abominable odour throughout that sacred edifice. It was in vain that old women who came to hear the sermons, although they were too deaf to catch a third part of them, brought smelling bottles, and other means of stifling their noses; still that dreadful charnel-house sort of smell would make itself most painfully and most disagreeably apparent.

Events now begin to move faster in the tradition of the best 'penny dreadful' serials. First, Tobias Ragg manages to escape from the madhouse while the owner is drunk; and Johanna Oakley – now calling herself 'Charley Green' – has learned what a dangerous man Sweeney Todd can be. Just when she begins to fear for her life, however, a note is thrust into her hand by a mysterious figure who slips quickly in and out of the shop. The note is from Sir Richard Brown who tells her he has learned of her mission – 'an enterprise which, considering your youth and your sex, should have been left to others' – but in the hope that it might lead to 'unmasking the villain', she will be kept under surveillance at all times.

Sweeney Todd is also becoming increasingly nervous that his crimes may be about to catch up with him. He has obtained a large sum of money for the string of pearls and feels it might be a good opportunity to leave London. But first there is the little matter of his partner, Mrs Lovett, who, it seems, has been demanding a bigger share of the spoils. Todd pays a visit to Bell Yard and promises to share with her the money he has received from the sale of the pearls.

'At this. Mrs Lovett rose and went into the shop,' the story goes on. 'The moment her back was turned, Todd produced a little bottle of poison and emptied it into the brandy decanter. He had just succeeded in his manoeuvre, and concealed the bottle again, when she appeared and flung herself into a chair.'

Sweeney Todd returns to Fleet Street satisfied he has settled with Mrs Lovett. A man is already waiting for him in the shop and tells him he is a wealthy farmer who has just made a profitable sale. Old habits die hard, and Todd determines to 'polish off' just one more victim. He dispatches his 'apprentice' Johanna on an errand and disappears into the next room to operate the chair a last time. When Todd reappears, however, the man has sprung nimbly from the seat and is waiting there to confront him. It is none other than Sir Richard Brown. The narrative continues:

"'Murderer!' shouted Sir Richard, in a voice that rung like the blast of a trumpet through the house. In an instant he sprang upon Sweeney Todd and grappled him by the throat. There was a short struggle and they were down upon the floor together. But Todd's wrists were suddenly laid hold of, and a pair of handcuffs most scientifically put upon them by the officer who had emerged from the cupboard where he had been concealed.

"'Secure him well, my man," said the magistrate, "and don't let him lay violent hands upon himself. We have discovered the secret of the chair and they mystery of the vaults. Thank God, we have stopped his career!"'

In Mrs Lovett's shop a short while later a final batch of pies appears from the underground cellar – and with it two shocks for the owner. Firstly, a man leaps from the tray to reveal to the customers that the pies are made of human flesh. Secondly, as Mrs Lovett clutches herself in a mixture of shock and agony, she realises the brandy that she had drunk earlier to steady her nerves must have been poisoned.

Into this scene of confusion arrives a party consisting of Sir Richard Brown, Colonel Jeffrey, Tobais Ragg and Johanna Oakley, now dressed in her own clothes once more. The young girl has clearly been unhappy about visiting the shop, until the moment Sir Richard points to the sorry figure of the pie-maker. It is her missing lover, Mark Ingestre. The pair cling together in a tearful reunion.

The String of Pearls then neatly ties up the loose ends of the story. Mrs Lovett did not recover consciousness from the dose of poison that Sweeney Todd had put in her bottle, while the barber himself 'passed that night in Newgate, and in due time a swinging corpse was all that remained of the barber of Fleet Street'.

The story added, 'Beneath the old church of St Dunstan were found the heads and bones of Todd's victims. As little as possible was said by the authorities about it. But it was supposed that some hundreds of persons must have perished in the frightful manner we have detailed.'

In the best tradition of Victorian romances, Mark and Johanna were married and young Tobias taken into their service. So ended the first version of the story of Sweeney Todd which evidently entertained the readers of *The People's Periodical* during the winter months of

1846-7. The anonymous author signed off his tale as simply as he had begun – and no doubt hurried round to Salisbury Square with the manuscript to collect his ten shilling fee.

'Johanna and Mark Ingestre,' he concluded, 'lived long and happily together, enjoying all the comforts of an independent existence – but they never forgot the strange and eventful circumstances connected with "The String of Pearls".'

The couple might, indeed, have suffered the fate of so many heroes and heroines of this kind of fiction by disappearing into oblivion – except for their association with the man called Sweeney Todd. Nor could the writer have had the least idea as he laid down his pen for the last time of the enduring effect his 'Romance' was to have on literature and, in particular, the theatre.

The Barber Fiend of Melodrama

The British public's appetite for exciting entertainment in the middle years of the nineteenth century can be summed up in a single word: voracious. During the first half of the century the population had increased from eight to sixteen million, and now that an ever-growing number of these people were semi-literate and even had a little money to spare in their pockets thanks to slightly improved wages, they wanted to forget their poor living conditions and hard, repetitive work in the evenings through escapist fare of one sort or another. The development of the printing press and its product the penny journal had provided one means of satisfying this demand. The theatrical 'melodrama' – which was to draw extensively on the latter – provided the second.

The melodrama as we understand it today emerged during the last years of the eighteenth century, flourished throughout the nineteenth, and died lingeringly in the first quarter of the twentieth century. It was produced in theatres of all descriptions from the vast stages of Drury Lane and Covent Garden to the most disreputable 'penny gafs' and travelling shows. As an art form, the melodrama has too often been written off contemptuously as sensational in tone, lacking in plot, and peopled by over-exaggerated characters of good or evil.

For myself, I believe the definition by Michael R. Booth in his study, *English Melodrama* (1965) comes closest to accurately defining the genre: 'Essentially, melodrama is a dream world inhabited by dream people and dream justice, offering audiences the fulfilment and satisfaction found only in dreams. An idealisation and simplification of the world of reality, it is in fact the world its audiences want but cannot get. In this world, life is uncomplicated, easy to understand, and immeasurably exciting. The world of melodrama is thus a world of certainties where confusion, doubt and perplexity are absent; a world of absolutes where after immense struggle and torment good triumphs over and punishes evil, and virtue receives tangible material rewards.'

In a nutshell, then, the melodrama provided its audiences with a diet of problems and disasters; although for the persecuted hero and tortured heroine, as well as the die-hard villain, there was only one inevitable outcome: good would always triumph over evil, no matter what the odds.

Melodramatic plays fell easily into two major categories: demonic and domestic. The first kind embraced all sorts of supernatural events and characters: devils, demons, vampires, ghosts and the like. The famous Gothic horror novels such as *The Castle of Otranto* by Horace Walpole (1764), Mrs Ann Radcliffe's *The Mysteries of Udolpho* (1794), and the notorious tale of the lecherous cleric, *The Monk* by Matthew Gregory Lewis (1796), had been the original inspiration for this type of production, and the plays drew heavily on their stock-in-trade locations such as ruined abbeys, moonlit churchyards, crumbling castles, haunted chambers, dark dungeons and so on. The plays all exploited the human emotion of 'fear-of-the-dark' and some of the characters were straight from nightmares, too. Of course, the demonic could on occasions stray into the domestic, but most theatre managements felt it was necessary to differentiate between the two to enable their audiences to be sure what they were getting. As a result, the two different categories developed.

The domestic melodrama dealt with real people in seemingly real situations – although the hero and heroine were probably far removed from the impoverished conditions of most of their audience. It was the emotions that were common to both, as Michael R. Booth has explained.

'Many domestic melodramas', he has written, 'do not have English settings and are at once removed from immediate reality. Their emotions, sentiments and situations, however, are perfectly familiar.'

These domestic melodramas were as likely to be placed in an idyllic rural setting as a grim city background. Yet there would invariably be the villain of the piece in the shape of a hardhearted squire or cruel landlord bent upon seduction, as well as the sorely tried hero and innocent heroine whose path to true love would be dogged by all the pitfalls of life. Crime was at the bottom of most of them – real crime, intended crime, or the crime associated in many people's minds with over-indulgence in drink, gambling or sex. At its most basic, the domestic melodrama utilised realistic raw materials processed into an end product of fantasy and wish fulfilment.

There were many real-life domestic crimes that made ideal material for the melodrama. A classic example was the story of Maria Marten, the molecatcher's daughter, who was seduced and murdered by the local squire, William Corder, in The Red Barn at Polstead in Suffolk in 1828. This drama, first recounted in the newspapers after Corder's arrest, trial and execution, soon became a long-running melodrama performed at all kinds of cheap theatres. It is still a favourite of repertory companies today.

Legendary figures like Robin Hood and Dick Turpin naturally co-mingled with more recent true stories, and all sorts of escapades – true, fictional and, frankly, sometimes unbelievable – were ascribed to them by the army of playwrights who kept the theatres supplied with scripts. As Maurice Wilson Disher says in *Blood and Thunder* (1949), his definitive study of Victorian melodrama and its origins, 'In cities where the increase in population was greatest, more theatres were needed, and more were provided with such enterprise that when Parliament freed the drama in 1843 (with the Licensing Act) the profession already had, what with the play-acting booths and saloons, all the freedom it needed. Blood and thunder flowed and rolled to the footlights everywhere.'

In the light of these facts, it is not difficult to understand why the story of *The String of Pearls* and, more particularly, the character of Sweeney Todd, should have been taken up by the theatre of melodrama. Nor, in truth, why the Demon Barber should soon become – and remain – one of the best-known characters in the theatre.

It was perhaps appropriate that the potential for adapting the Sweeney Todd story for the stage should have first been appreciated by probably the greatest of all London's melodrama theatres, The Britannia in High Street, Hoxton. This was a theatre management for which Thomas Peckett Prest had produced material during the years 1841 to 1849 – a point to which I shall return shortly.

Today, unhappily, The Britannia is no more. But this former tavern which became one of the most popular cheap theatres of its time, has been immortalised in Charles Dickens's series of essays about London,

The Uncommercial Traveller, published in 1861. Although, of course, with the passing of time, it is impossible to recreate the vanished playhouse – its flickering lights picking out the flamboyant gestures of the actors, and the noisy audiences shouting their cheers and boos between mouthfuls of beer and fried fish and potatoes – some mention of it is important. For this was, after all, where the greatest of all the monsters of melodrama, Sweeney Todd, first trod the boards.

Fortunately, something of the magic of the 'Brit' has been captured in print by Barton Baker, a regular visitor to the theatre, in his book, *The London Stage,* published in 1889:

'The Britannia – once called a saloon, but now a theatre – has only known one management, the founder, Sam Lane, and he has been succeeded by his widow, who still directs its destinies. Actors enter the theatre in their youth and remain there until age incapacitates them, or until they have strutted and fretted their last hour upon the stage of life. Authors wrote exclusively for this house, and it was the last to give up its own peculiar style of drama for second-hand West End pieces. Until very recently, its pantomimes enjoyed the longest runs in London, and are usually mounted with exceptional brilliancy.'

Hoxton High Street was itself a well-known centre for entertainment. Prior to the opening of the 'Brit', another hostelry, the Pimlico, where live entertainment was provided had stood on the same site for generations. The Britannia opened as a theatre on Easter Monday, 1841, offering, 'Variety, grand concert, opera, vaudeville and laughable farce' with 'neither talent nor expense spared' at prices ranging from 6d (six pence) in the gallery to one shilling in the front stalls, 'with which a refreshment ticket is given'.

It was after the passing of the Licensing Act in 1843 that the 'Brit' turned to melodrama. So successful did this policy prove that in 1858 the old saloon was closed down and the premises were enlarged to form a colossal new theatre which could hold up to 5,000 people.

The names of just a few of the melodramas which the Britannia staged over the years are a clear indication as to why it could draw huge audiences from all over the metropolis: *The Mother's Dying Child, or Woman's Fate; Pure as Driven Snow, or Tempted in Vain; Taking The Veil* and *The Headless Horseman* to name just four. So it was surely with the usual sense of anticipation that the crowds streamed into the theatre on the night of 1 March, 1847 for the first performance of *The*

String of Pearls, or The Barber Fiend of Fleet Street. Their interest may also have been heightened by the announcement below the title on the posters that the story was 'taken from the much admired Tale of that name in *Lloyd's People's Periodical';* and even further whetted by the admission, 'For dramatic effect, and to adapt the story to general taste, some alterations have been judiciously made, enhancing its interest.'

Charles Dickens, who attended the 'Brit' on just such a night, has provided a graphic picture of the collection of noisy, colourful and uninhibited folk who made up a typical audience:

'We were a motley assemblage of people, and we had a good many boys and young men among us; we had also many girls and young women. To represent, however, that we did not include a very great number, and a very fair proportion of family groups, would be to make a gross mis-statement. Such groups were to be seen in all parts of the house. In the boxes and stalls particularly, they were composed of persons of very decent appearance, who had many children with them.

'Among our dresses there were most kinds of shabby and greasy wear, and much fustian and corduroy that was neither sound nor fragrant. The caps of our young men were mostly of the limp character, and we who wore them, slouched, high-shouldered, into our places with our hands in our pockets, and occasionally twisted our cravats about our necks like eels, and occasionally tied them down our breasts like links of sausages, and occasionally had a screw in our hair over each cheek bone with a slight thief-flavour in it.

'Besides prowlers and idlers, we were mechanics, dock-labourers, costermongers, petty tradesmen, small clerks, milliners, stay-makers, shoe-binders, shop workers, poor workers in a hundred highways and byways. Most of us – on the whole, the majority – were not at all clean, and not at all choice in our lives or conversation. But we had all come together in a place where our convenience was well consulted, and where we were well looked after, to enjoy an evening's entertainment in common. We were not going to loose any part of what we had paid for, through anybody's caprice, and as a community we had a character to lose. So, we were closely attentive, and kept excellent order. And let the man or boy who did otherwise instantly get out from this place, or we would put him out with the greatest expedition.'

The melodrama for that night of 1 March, *The String of Pearls,* was the handiwork of one of the theatre's busiest authors, George Dibdin

Pitt, although he received no specific credit on the hand-bill. The fact that *The People's Periodical* was mentioned seems a clear indication that the serial had been popular with readers and the management were keen to associate their production with that success.

George Dibdin Pitt (1799-1855) came from a family who had been associated with the London theatre for many years, and while their fortunes appear to have varied from time to time, they were never long out of work or in financial need like a great many other people in the profession in the nineteenth century. George's mother was an actress and his father a song writer, and he naturally graduated into theatrical life when still a young man. He first tried acting with only modest success, then became a stage manager, before finally discovering his true métier as a playwright. His first drama was a piece entitled *My Own Blue Bell* performed at the Surrey Theatre in 1831.

The real upturn in Pitt's fortunes occurred in 1841 when Sam Lane took him on as the resident playwright at the newly opened Britannia. His skill at quickly devising melodramas around topics of interest seems to have already been well established – perhaps his biggest success having been *The Eddystone Elf,* a drama about a sea monster that haunts the famous lighthouse, produced at Sadler's Wells in 1834 – and within a very short time he was averaging at least one new play per month.

Like other dramatists providing material for the cheap theatres, Pitt got many of his plots from the penny journals – sometimes lifting stories virtually wholesale and making only minimal changes to the author's original dialogue. There was, as I have mentioned earlier, no copyright in operation then to prevent this piracy.

The many publications from Salisbury Square were rich sources of material, and there is evidence that writers like Thomas Peckett Prest sometimes offered their services to theatre owners in the hope of getting a little financial recompense from their tales rather than stand by and see them stolen for nothing. Indeed, we know that Prest had an agreement with Sam Lane during the 1840s, and it is my belief that he played a part in seeing *The String of Pearls* transferred to the stage, perhaps even lending George Dibdin Pitt a hand in the actual dramatisation. I base this belief on two things. Firstly, that the stage presentation of *The String of Pearls* opened on 1 March, *three weeks* before the serial reached its final episode in *The People's Periodical;* and although there are differences in the text of the serial and the play, the crucial closing episodes are much the same in both. These are surely developments that only Prest could have known and must have shared with Pitt – if he did not actually write some of the drama itself. Secondly – and here the evidence is more circumstantial – it is known that Pitt produced twenty-six plays during 1847: a total that even in those prolific days it seems hard to believe he could have achieved without some form of assistance. It therefore seems probable to me that Pitt and Prest pooled their talents on this occasion, too. The fact the play is not specifically credited to Pitt – as most of his other works were – is also a factor not without significance.

Although a copy of the playbill for the first performance of *The String of Pearls* is still in existence at the British Museum, the names of the cast probably meant a great deal more to the patrons of the 'Brit' than they do to us today. However, they are worth mentioning because of their part in the launching of Sweeney Todd on the stage.

The Demon Barber himself was played by Mark Howard, who had starred as the villain in a number of melodramas, and was subsequently to become known as 'The Fiendish Figaro'. Indeed, Howard repeated the role several times during his career, and is credited with having originated a number of the mannerisms still associated with the part.

The role of Sweeney Todd's partner in crime, Mrs Lovett, was pioneered by a Miss Maria Hamilton, although it seems she did not retain the role for long. Most early recollections of the play state that the pie-maker was 'seductively played by Mrs Emma Atkinson', another familiar figure in melodrama at the time and the mother of the famous Sadler's Wells actress, Ann Atkinson. It was Mrs Lovett's fate to be shot by her paramour in this version, instead of either taking her own life or being poisoned.

Interestingly, too, the cruelly-wronged apprentice, Tobias Ragg, was actually played by a diminutive young woman, Mrs Hudson Kirby; while the part of the determined Colonel Jeffrey was taken by another of the 'Brit's' regular actors, Mr J. Mordaunt. Sam Sawford was the mysterious Jarvis Williams – revealed in the last scene to be the missing Mark Ingestre – with Miss C Braham as the beautiful Johanna Oakley.

These, then, were the players who gave the story of Sweeney Todd its first performance in March 1847, establishing a tradition that has continued to this day. Unfortunately, however, it was not the custom

of the London theatre critics to attend productions at the Britannia –
indeed, most tended to scorn all melodramas – and only a single, eyewitness report has survived of an early production of the George
Dibdin Pitt-Thomas Peckett Prest production. The account appears in
Thomas W. Erie's book, *Letters From A Theatrical Scene Painter*,
published in 1880. Evidence in the book suggests it must describe one
of the earlier performances of the play, probably about 1850. I think
it is well worth reprinting in full.

An evening at the Britannia during the run of 'The String of Pearls; *or,*
The Barber Fiend of Fleet Street', *was to sup full of horrors. In the vulgar
tongue of Hoxton and elsewhere, a full supper is called a 'tightener'. The
expression is coarse, no doubt, yet suggestive. Abominably so. Going to see*
The Barber Fiend *was a tightener of horrors, like a visit to the small room
at Madame Tussaud's.*

   *The plot was as follows. The barber Fiend murders in succession all his
customers who come to him to be shaved, and then, by way of utilising
them to the utmost possible extent, as well as of conveniently disposing of
their bodies, makes them into pies, upon which such of the characters as we
are left to carry through the business of the piece, are regaled. A series of
effects is produced by successive discoveries in the pies of what may be called
'internal evidence' of the true nature of their ingredients. Thus, one of the
consumers finds in the first instance a woman's hair. This is not viewed as
a circumstance of much gravity, since it is a matter of common experience
that long hairs have an intrusive tendency which induces them to present
themselves in combination with most alimentary substances. From buns,
for example, they are as inseparable as grit.*

   *But to return to the Barber's pies. The discovery of the hair is
followed by that of a thumb nail, which appears to give rise to some
indistinct, but uneasy, misgivings in the breast of the consumer. He
pursues his meal with reflective hesitation, and with a zest which has
now been obviously impaired by the operation of disquieting mental
influences. The startling revelation of a brass button attached to a
fragment of material substance of some kind or other which bears the
aspect of having once formed a constituent portion of somebody or
other's leather breeches, proves what is called 'a staggerer', and brings
the repast to an abrupt and uncomfortable conclusion. The terrors of the
scene culminate in the discovery of a full and detailed account of the*

whole matter set fourth on the paper in which the pies had been wrapped. The narrative in question is accompanied by strictures on the conduct of the murderer, ably drawn up by his victims, and a free and explicit confession by himself is also appended to the document. At this point a torrent of fiddles is let loose, which rasp away for some moments with an energy worthy of the crisis.

The Barber is then taken into custody. But not by policemen. Not a bit of it! The R B management knows better than that. Police constables, no doubt, constitute a highly respectable and estimable body of men. Still, when they march in with the mechanical precision of automata, as stiff as a procession of animated lamp-posts, and with countenances fraught with utter unmeaningness, they present, it must be confessed, the very essence of the unpicturesque in effect. And their plain, matter-of-fact truncheons are but silent and ineffective accessories to a situation. No. A party of supers rush in, attired in the uniforms in which they are acustomed to 'do' the Swedish army in Charles the Twelfth, and let off their muskets with signal intrepidity, firing earnestly upwards, as though anxious to hit some bird or other object which they must be supposed to have descried flitting about up among the gas patterns. This light fusillade, incidentally, brings about the desirable result of creating a strong smell of gunpowder, and the noise throws a collection of urchins at the door of the theatre, who cannot muster their sixpence for the gallery, into paroxysms of excitement to know what is going on inside. Of all the various sad forms of human destitution, perhaps the most affecting to contemplate is that of small boys who hang night after night about the doors of theatres but can't afford to go in.

The apprehension of the wicked barber necessarily brings the drama to its conclusion, and at this point, therefore, all the murdered characters reappear. If it be objected that the supposition of his guilt is weakened by, not to say is absolutely inconsistent with, the bodily presence of his victims – the ipsissima corpora delictorum – all as right and tight as can be, the answer is that the claims of the final tableau are paramount. The scene is illuminated with red fire. An explanation of the propriety of this enrichment of the tableau is probably to be sought in the notion of its being in some degree typical of the subject-matter of the piece, since it is not within ordinary experience that the action of retributive justice is attended by any such meteoric phenomena. The whole of the characters then joined in a patriotic song, in which the invasion panic, and the discomfiture of the enemy by the gallantry of the Hoxton volunteers, together with any other points which may happen to be of general interest to the community at that particular moment, are very neatly and happily touched off.

Now if that isn't a 'strong' piece, pray what is? If the reader does not agree with me in so characterising it, I should then be glad to be put in possession of his views as to what is a strong piece. Surely the conversion of one half of the characters in the drama into animal sustenance for the other half is an incident of a complexion sufficiently decided to arrest attention. In the ultimate denouement of the plot more formidable and perplexing difficulties have to be encountered than even in the case of a certain novel which was published in parts in one of the penny awfuls some time ago. In that instance, the author, on getting into a tiff with the editor of the periodica, brought the story which was in course of publication to an abrupt and absurd conclusion by taking all his characters out in a boat to a spot about midway between Dover and Calais, and there upsetting them into the sea, and drowning them like a litter of mongrel puppies. Subsequently, however, being desirous to publish his work in a separate form on his own account, he became obliged to fish them all up again from the bottom of the sea, and set them to work out a proper conclusion as best they might. But in The Barber Fiend *half the dramatis personae have to be resuscitated after mastication and digestion by the other half.*

I must say the Barber was well played and as dramatic impressions are so strong with me, I should not go out of my way to get my hair cut in Fleet Street just at present. The uncomfortable atmosphere of suspicion and distrust which already envelops the rations of opaque slime and gristle conventionally known as mutton pies is amply sufficient of itself, without the addition of any further unpleasant misgivings which might be suggested by The Barber Fiend, *to discourage one from partaking of those ambiguous delicacies. When I was at school, a man who sold mutton pies to the boys went the way of all piemen, and his son succeeded to the business. It was currently reported and believed that* no funeral ever took place. *This, under the circumstances, was a tremendous fact. For it afforded room for surmising that the expression that the deceased had 'gone the way of all flesh' was pregnant with unusual significance. If it had been stated that he had 'gone to his last home', his place of final rest and his son's mutton pies, might, not impossibly, under the particular conditions of his disappearance, have proved to be convertible terms.*

It was a disappointment that there was no call for the author, as I should have liked to have seen the party. His cast of mind must be a sort of combination of Lady Macbeth's with that of the editor of The Newgate Calendar *[sic]. He must reside in some spectral and gloomy scene, such as Gower Street, or the immediate vicinity of Cold Bath Field's Prison, where the picture of desolate and dreary waste which is ever presented to his view is unrelieved by any stray gleam of a cheerful tint. Moreover, the conception and composition of* The Barber Fiend *must have taken place in his moments of acute indigestion. Perverted fancies of the imagination like this are usually the result of functional disorder in the system.*

Joking apart, I think that the representation of such a mass of unnatural and repulsive horrors is extremely wrong and pernicious, and the subsequent astonishing resuscitation of the victims does little to rectify it. If the Drama be 'holding the mirror up to nature', it should also be remembered that there is such a thing, and a very real and common thing too, as holding nature up to the mirror. For the contemplation, or vivid description, of an art of wickedness, frequently, as is perfectly known, inoculates weak minds with an irresistible impulse to do the same kind of thing. It was in this course that Courvoisier, who murdered his master, Lord William Russell, declared himself to have been brought to the gallows, and there have been many similar instances. Besides which, it isn't the pleasantest thing in the world to sit for an hour or two looking at murders, although they are but sham ones, nor is it in good taste to have too many of them on the stage.

It is doubtful whether the majority of the first night audience of *The String of Pearls* as they poured noisily out of the theatre shared Thomas Erie's reservations about the play. They were, after all, in the main people who were hardened to tales of crime and death, who enjoyed descriptions of murder and killings, and could take violence and passion in their stride. They may not have had Erie's sensibilities, either, but they would have agreed that the idea of a drama about a man who murdered his customers and turned them into meat pies was definitely unusual: certainly something to make you think twice the next time you decided to visit a barber or buy a tasty meat pie!

Perhaps, too, there were some members of the audience that night – and in the nights to come – who might have remembered the story of the original 'Barber Fiend of Fleet Street' which had been a part of London gossip for half a century. Indeed prommently printed on the bills outside the theatre – just beneath the title of the play – were the words, FOUNDED ON FACT. But no matter how many saw that statement, or even bothered to consider whether it was intended as some sort of justification for the horrors, Thomas Erie's protest that putting on such a story was 'wrong and pernicious' fell on deaf ears. The Demon Barber had now made his bow in literature and in the theatre and would never be removed from centre stage again.

16

Idol of The Rogue's Gallery

By the end of the nineteenth century, Sweeney Todd was a firmly established favourite in print and on the stage. The life and crimes of the Demon Barber had been novelised and serialised several times more, all the versions drawing heavily on *The String of Pearls;* while the Britannia's theatrical version had been similarly appropriated by other places of entertainment. As Maurice Disher has written in *Blood and Thunder,* 'Henceforward, Sweeney Todd would rank in the rogue's gallery of the sensation-loving public as second only to that perpetual idol of the nineteenth-century masses, Dick Turpin.'

There was clearly something about Sweeney Todd which struck a chord with audiences, and he became the 'villain you love to hate' in print and on the stage. Aside from the public's mixture of fascination and revulsion at the hints of cannibalism, the Demon Barber's notoriety was no doubt helped by the timing of his appearance when novels and plays were cross-fertilising each other to a very considerable extent. As Wilkie Collins expressed it in a preface to his novel, *Basil* (1852): 'The novel and the play are twin-sisters in the family of Fiction: the one is a drama narrated, as the other is a drama acted. All the strong and deep emotions that the playwright is privileged to excite, the novelist is privileged to excite also.' This view is also shared by a modern commentator, Richard D. Altick in his book, *Victorian Studies in Scarlet* (1972), where he writes, 'Such is probably the case with the most memorable of the horrific stories that became part of Victorian popular lore – the tale of Sweeney Todd, the mad barber of Fleet Street, whose penny shaving shop was equipped with a trapdoor beside [sic] the barber chair.'

The number of emphemeral publications and little theatre versions of Todd's story which were produced during the Victorian era will probably never be known. Certainly the British Museum has very few copies, and in some instances only the titles of the stories and plays have survived at all. Commenting on this, Montague Summers wrote in *A Gothic Bibliography*, 'There have been innumerable melodramatic adaptations of Sweeney Todd, many of which were never printed and only hastily made for the very minor theatres. Nonetheless, in one or other of the adaptations, the play has been frequently played in London and throughout the provinces ever since.'

As Summers suggests, what all these productions served to achieve was the continuing fame of Sweeney Todd.

The original stage production of *The String of Pearls* at the Britannia certainly continued for some years – alternating with both new melodramas and revivals of some of the old favourites. It was also revised several times to highlight the villainy of Sweeney Todd and remove some of the extraneous characters who cluttered up the original. It was, after all, the Fiend of Fleet Street that the paying public at the 'Brit' came to see.

Some later versions of the story included a bibulous clergyman bent on seduction; a large Beefeater from the Tower of London given to roars of hearty laughter at inappropriate moments; and a clutch of comic policemen. A further alteration in 1860 had the villain being foiled not by a hero, but by the principal comedian – a device which has subsequently been worked to death by other playwrights.

As the century drew to a close, Sweeney Todd even began to appear as a character in other plays, too. Sometimes he was just a subsidiary villain, introduced as a crowd-puller when the mere mention of his name was enough to guarantee boos and hisses from the audience; while in a number of the cheaper travelling shows and 'penny gaffs' he remained a star in his own right – though he was often attributed with even more horrendous crimes than either real life, books or theatre had attributed to him.

Probably the next major stageplay to feature his activities was produced by Frederick Hazelton in 1862. It is clear from the title that the author had his priorities right and knew exactly who the public were coming to see. *Sweeney Todd, the Barber of Fleet Street,* he called his version, adding: *or, The String of Pearls.*

Hazelton's new melodrama was in three acts and actually began where the other stories left off with Todd being arrested outside his shop and conveyed to Newgate. From here he escapes intent on murdering Mrs Lovett whom he believes has informed on him to the authorities. The play was climaxed by a fight between the pair which ended with the Demon Barber falling through his own trapdoor and being consumed by flames. The production was first staged at the Bower Saloon in Lambeth and ran there successfully for some time before its transfer to the Pavillion Theatre in Mile End. The man who played Sweeney Todd in this production was George Yates whose performance was compared to that of Mark Howard. A critic, Henry C. Porter, writing in 1902, said 'Yates took the part of the Barber Fiend, and made it very popular among the patrons of the fourth-rate playhouses.' A recent historian, Michael Kilgarrif in his *Golden Age of Melodrama* (1974) adds further: 'The most celebrated Demon Barber of the century was George Yates of the Pavillion, Mile End, who, with his large-sized wife, Harriet Clifton, as Mrs Lovett, made as fearsome a duo as a horror addict could wish for in a month of Bloody Sundays.'

Another actor who made something of a speciality of the role of Sweeney Todd was Cecil Pitt, who had appeared in a minor role as the keeper of a madhouse in the first production at the Britannia. He was actually the younger brother of George Dibdin Pitt and so may well have been able to claim a special inside knowledge of the part. Cecil Pitt also appeared as Todd in another version of the story written by Matt Wilkinson which, although it again followed the original storyline, made more of the Demon Barber as an evil seducer of young girls. Daringly, for its time, it had Todd leching after his assistant 'Charley Green', apparently unaware that the 'boy' was actually the beautiful Johanna Oakley in disguise.

It would be wrong, however, to think that the play was only an attraction to the lower classes of London: Charles Dickens, who has so graphically described a visit to the Britannia, was just one of many folk from the upper and middle classes who considered it an exciting night out to go to the cheap theatres. It is almost entirely due to the fact that the newspapers of the time considered it beneath their dignity to write about such productions, that we have been left with the idea that these were just the entertainments of the poor. That gentleman of the theatre, John W. Hales, made no bones about his predeliction for such fare when writing in *Notes & Queries* in August, 1901: 'In the year 1859 I well remember going with my old college friend Walter Besant, who was to become so famous, to a performance called, *The String of*

Pearls; or, The Barber Fiend of Fleet Street. I forget whether the theatre at which it was played was the Standard in Shoreditch or the Britannia, Hoxton; but I think it was the Britannia. Certainly our blood was curdled, *steteruntque comoe.'*

It is interesting to note that although by common consent, Pitt's play about Todd was the best on offer, the Britannia felt obliged to change the title as the competition from other sources hotted up. Montague Summers in his *Gothic Bibliography* tells us that it was 'changed to "Sweeney Todd" (often with the sub-title, "The Demon Barber of Fleet Street") and was continually acted until the Britannia as a theatre closed its doors.'

Mr Summers also adds, 'There have been innumerable melodramatic adaptations of Sweeney Todd, many of which were never printed and only hastily made for the very minor theatres. . .In one or other of the adaptations, the play has been frequently played in London and throughout the provinces ever since.'

It was not until this century, however, that the actor whose name is still most closely associated with the role of Sweeney Todd first played the role on the stage and then succesfully transplanted the Demon Barber to film. His name was, appropriately, Tod Slaughter.

Slaughter, the 'master of melodrama' as he is remembered, probably did more than anyone to bridge Sweeney Todd's fame from the Victorian era to recent times. His name became synonymous with the role, and when he died in February 1956 it was claimed that he had appeared in the part over 4,000 times on the stage, as well as in the classic screen version, in a career that spanned over fifty years.

* * *

It is a popular misconception that Tod Slaughter was the first person to play the Demon Barber on film in 1936. This is not, in fact, the case: Sweeney Todd made his debut on the screen during the silent era in a comedy burlesque made by New Era Films in 1926. Called simply *Sweeney Todd,* this short, silent movie bore more similarity to a Keystone Cops farce than the grisly tale of the Fleet Street murderer. It was ostensibly based on George Dibdin Pitt's play, but the screenwriter, P. L. Mannock took quite a few liberties with the story, while the director, George Dewhurst played most of the action for laughs. The only actor credited in the picture is G. A. Baughan who appeared as Sweeney Todd. The film was apparently premiered at the unlikely venue of the Cinematograph Garden Party in 1926! Sadly, no copy appears to have survived.

The second picture, made two years later by Stoll Films, was a much more substantial effort, and the uncredited scriptwriter drew on the work of both Pitt and Frederick Hazelton, although his version did vary in one significant way. Initially, the writer stuck to the theme of the Demon Barber who slits the throats of his customers, steals their valuables and then throws the bodies into a cellar where they are collected by the widow Lovett for making into pies for her cooked meat shop next door. But instead of being arrested and executed for his crimes, this Sweeney Todd – played by Moore Marriott –awakes in his bed to find the whole thing has been a bad dream.

The reason for this *volte farce* has never been satisfactorily explained. Did the producer, Harry Rowson, feel the original story was too much for sensitive stomachs in the twenties? Or were Stoll Films afraid that the subject matter might prove too revolting for the public who were then just getting over reading the horrific details of the arrest and trial of Fritz Hartman, a German homosexual killer, who had murdered some fifty young men and boys between 1918 and 1924 and sold their flesh for human consumption in his cooked meat shop? Whatever the reason, Moore Marriott nevertheless made quite a success of his role, although he is, of course, better remembered for playing the hoary old rustic in the Will Hay comedies of the thirties and forties. His co-stars were Zoe Palmer and Charles Ashton as die hero and heroine, Johanna Oakley and Mark Ingestre.

It is, however, the Tod Slaughter version of *Sweeney Todd, The Demon Barber of Fleet Street,* made with sound and in black and white by Ambassador Pictures in 1936, that remains the best known movie to date.

Tod Slaughter had, as I mentioned earlier, been playing the role for many years in theatres throughout the British Isles, but the movie directed by the versatile George King assured him of a place in the ranks of the cinema's great horror stars.

Seeing the picture today, Tod Slaughter can easily be accused of an over-the-top performance; but there is no denying the ghoulish relish with which he tackles the role, nor the fact that the picture has now become a cult classic – particularly in America where it is favourite on college campuses and at film festivals. In this version, the scriptwriters, Frederick Hayward and H. F. Maltby, took George Dibdin Pitt's play as their starting point; but made a great deal more of the razor-slashing, throat-cutting and human pie-making elements of the tale than anyone before them had done. Tod Slaughter, for his part, was said to have become so immersed in the role that he genuinely frightened some of his fellow actors when they had to sit in the revolving chair. A youthful Bruce Seton played Mark Ingestre, with Eve Lister as Johanna and Stella Rho as a malevolent Mrs Lovett.

The film also has an interesting framing story which begins and ends the movie and may well have been added during post-production for reasons that can now only be guessed at. At the start, a customer is seen arriving at a barber's shop in contemporary Fleet Street. Here he is regaled with the legend of Sweeney Todd who inhabited the same premises over a hundred and fifty years before as the picture fades into the story. During the epilogue, the customer becomes increasingly upset by the gorey tale and suddenly sneaks out of the shop and is last seen running down the road towards the safety of St Paul's!

Like Basil Rathbone as Sherlock Holmes, Tod Slaughter was destined thereafter to be forever associated with the part of Sweeney Todd – although he could well claim to have established the Demon Barber in yet another medium of entertainment.

The actor was born Norman Carter Slaughter in Newcastle-upon-Tyne in 1885, and his road to stardom had been a long and hard one. Beginning with walk-on parts, followed by small roles in provincial rep, it was not for some years that he realised that his talent lay in playing villains, especially in revivals of the old melodramas.

Slaughter established his reputation in the years immediately after the First World War when he took over as actor-manager of the old Elephant & Castle Theatre in London, and there staged a whole series of blood and thunder melodramas including *The Murder in the Red Barn, Jack Sheppard, Spring Heeled Jack* and, of course, *Sweeney Todd.* He repeated a number of these roles in both radio and film adaptations which brought his name to an even wider audience.

After the Second World War, Tod Slaughter continued to be a popular box office draw at theatres throughout the country, starring in a number of Grand Guignol plays, of which *Sweeney Todd* remained far and away the most successful. According to his friends, he was a demon for work – indeed he listed his hobbies in *Who's Who* as 'gardening and work' – and continued to appear on stage right up to the time of his death. Sadly, although he enjoyed a long and happy marriage to the actress Jenny Lind (whom he had 'slain' in virtually every conceivable manner during their stage partnership), he was rather less successful in running his financial affairs, and three years before his death a receiving order for bankruptcy was issued against him.

'After fifty years in the theatre,' he said ruefully after the court hearing, 'with a completely clean record, this is *humiliating*'.

When Tod Slaughter died on 19 February, 1956, the press had certainly not forgotten his glory days. The *Daily Mail,* for instance, spread the news across three columns under the heading THE SMILING VILLAIN NOBODY CONDEMNED, while even *The Times* subtitled its obituary, 'The Demon Barber of the Stage'. The *Mail's* entertainment writer, Cecil Wilson, expressed the feelings of millions when he wrote:

'Tod Slaughter, the most lovable multi-murderer on the British stage, the villain with the comedian's face, who immortalised the crimes of Sweeney Todd, the Demon Barber, died in his sleep yesterday. He had appeared in *The Murder in the Red Barn* on Saturday night. The man who, in private life, could not bring himself to strangle a chicken, would have been 71 next month, and murder most foul has been his speciality for most of his 51 years in the theatre.

'He had 340 plays in his repertoire – mostly gruesome affairs in which the villain was always of the blackest, the hero the noblest, and the heroine the sweetest – and he was always the grateful target for every boo and hiss.'

The *News Chronicle* headlined its report DEMON BARBER WAS LAST OF HIS KIND, and said, 'Over four thousand times as Sweeney Todd he severed jugulars and brought horror to the faces of his audiences as rich-red cochineal spurted from his property razor. Many people in and out of the theatre called him Sweeney because he was so identified with the role.'

The newspaper noted that Tod Slaughter had made a 78rpm record with his wife, Jenny Lynn, of *Sweeney Todd,* which 'offered a somewhat stronger rendition than was deemed permissible in the cinema.' *The News Chronicle* added that he had reprised his role in two short films for Pathe in 1936 and 1938 and a short vignette entitled,

Bothered by a Beard in 1945. Two years before his death he had once again appeared as the infamous character reciting a monologue in *Puzzle Corner* with all his old relish.

The appropriately named John Barber of the *Daily Express* – who also happened to be a friend of the performer – declared 'no living actor curdled more blood or stormed more barns than Norman Carter Slaughter'.

He continued: 'His flickering eyebrows and throaty chuckle had gloated over red ketchup spouting from countless jugulars. His unforgettable cry, "Oh, I'd love to polish you off!" addressed to inter-rupters on average 12 times a performance, six nights a week, made him a legend long before his death.

'Yet he was an artist. He did not just rant through a bloodstained repertoire. No one was quicker to sense an audience's mood. When he carved, he cut clean and sure with a gleaming knife. I can still hear him, as he stepped across the road to the theatre, "Coming in, John? I'm killing them well in the oven tonight!"'

17

Mystery of The Demon Barber of Broadway

It is very evident today that the main reason why the *facts* of Sweeney Todd's life have become so obscure is the flood of fiction that has been published ever since 'The String of Pearls' appeared in Edward Lloyd's publication, *The People's Periodical & Family Library,* back in November 1846 and launched the interest in the serial killer that has continued for 160 years. This torrent of words has included serials, novels, paperbacks, pamphlets, even comic strips and a graphic novel that have come from writers and publishers in Britain, France and the United States. A glance through the library of these works – many of which have claimed to be 'based on authentic events' – throws a fascinating light on the development of the phenomenon as well as revealing a remarkable company of writers who, like the creators of the Lloyd serial, have contributed in one way or the other to the mystery surrounding the saga.

Perhaps it should come as no real surprise to discover in such a relentless age of plagiarism in print and the theatre as the Nineteenth Century, that a playwright was responsible for the first novelisation of the story of Sweeney Todd in 1862. Frederick Hazleton (c. 1825-1890) who adapted the Lloyd original for the Bower Saloon in Lambeth (later the Royal Stangate Theatre) wrote a ten thousand word adaptation under the much more evocative title of *Sweeney Todd, the Demon Barber of Fleet Street.* The primary target for this penny publication was theatre goers and every copy was embellished with a dramatic illustration of Todd dispatching one of his victims in the revolving chair.

Hazleton was a journeyman writer who had spent the previous decade churning out stories for the 'Penny Dreadfuls' or creating plays for the smaller London theatres. Much of his work was published by one of Lloyd's keenest rivals, George Vickers, who had offices in Angel

Court, just off the Strand. There are scant details about Hazleton's life, and in the few reference works that mention him at all – such as Montague Summers – he is listed as the author of the popular serial, *Charley Wagg, The New Jack Sheppard,* a bloodthirsty tale of villainy in the London underworld that appeared in 1861.

It seems likely that Hazleton came upon the Sweeney Todd legend in the early 1860s and wrote his three-act play shortly after. The all-action melodrama starring the rumbustuous George Yates went on to enjoy one of the longest and most profitable runs recorded at the Bower. In the announcements for the play, it is stated that the production was 'Founded on the popular work of the same tile by Fred Hazleton Esq., author *of Charley Wag* & etc' Whether he had actually written the book *before* the play is open to conjecture, as this kind of promotional material was one of the most popular ways of selling penny versions of plays. What is beyond dispute, though, is that the grubbily printed pamphlet was 'For sale in Bookshops, Newsagents and Theatres' with the enticing word 'Demon' inserted into Sweeney's job description. Whether Hazleton, or his publisher, George Vickers, gave it this title, they had unconsciously provided the soubriquet by which the story of the serial killer would forever be known.

What Hazleton did in his version was to extract the figure of Todd from the Lloyd narrative and make him the character around which everything revolves. The young lovers, Mark Ingestrie and Johanna Oakley, are relegated to minor roles: though Johanna proves to be more than the usual simpering Victorian heroine when she disguises herself as a boy to become Sweeney's apprentice in the hope of discovering what has happened to her missing fiance. Liberated heroines such as her were few and far between at this time, and her actions give another special element to Hazleton's version.

The author also did his best to paint Sweeney Todd as an archfiend who appals the reader, at the same time seizing his interest. Like all hack writers – perpetually hard up – Hazleton probably had to produce the book quickly and it shows evident signs of haste in several parts. Yet as a scriptwriter, he knew how to construct fast-paced and engrossing dialogue and as a Londoner had the personal knowledge to paint a vivid picture of the locality in which the story is set. Furthermore, he writes with the assurance of someone who believed the story to be true, and it is to be regretted that he made no mention of his sources.

By a stroke of good fortune during my research, I found a book written by a man who actually saw Hazleton's *Sweeney Todd* performed on the stage. He was Henry Chance Newton, a London journalist who wrote a column under the pen name 'Carados' for the weekly paper, *The Referee*. Later, in his memoirs. *Crime and the Drama, or Dark Deeds Dramatized,* published in 1927, he recalled his impressions of the play:

'I first saw the Sweeney Todd drama when I was a boy and on the first occasion I remember I saw it from a front seat and was so terrified that I had to hide under the seat! A little later I got used to this terrible tragedy; and from that time I often saw it from behind the scenes, that is from the wings or the prompt box. In all I saw the drama many, many times.'

More significantly, Chance followed his reporter's nose to investigate the background to the story and took the opportunity to disabuse sceptical readers that that the Demon Barber was nothing more than a fictional character:

'Having studied Sweeney Todd ever since I could read or sit at the play, or toddle behind the scenes, I have come to the conclusion that the story is based upon a real criminal of the time who operated on the very spot where Sweeney's shop was supposed to be. Having been brought up, as it were, to regard this bloodthirsty blackguard as a real person, naturally I too made it my business to find out the site of the emporium wherein he committed his dark deeds. Now this shop site was, I found, that which became utilised in after-times and up to a few years ago as Craig's fish restaurant, a few doors on the City side from the Church of St Dunstan's, Fleet Street.'

Within three years of the success of the Demon Barber melodrama in London, a pirate version, *Sweeney Todd, or, The Ruffian Barber* was on sale across the Atlantic for American readers. The publishers were H. Long & Brother of Nassau Street in New York, specialists in 'Cheap Publications and Magazines' who unashamedly plagiarised the work of both popular American and European writers. The founder, Henry Long, was an entrepreneur in the same mould as Edward Lloyd and went for his target audience with early titles such as *The Slave of the Lake* and *The Spirit Rappers,* before casting covetous eyes on the work of English writers like G.W.M. Reynolds (1814-1879) who had made *his* reputation with imitations of Dickens

(Pickwick Abroad) and salacious serials like *The Mysteries of London*, which Louis James has described as 'the *Forever Amber* of early Victorian fiction.' Henry Long recruited a stable of writers to work on copying Edward Lloyd's most successful 'Penny Dreadfuls' for sale at 50 cents or a dollar a copy.

One of Long's most prolific writers was Harry Hazel [Jones] (1814-1889) – another dipsomaniac and spend-thrift like Thomas Prest – whose forte was historical sagas including *Yankee Jack* (1852), *The Gold Seekers* (1853), *The Cobbler of Gotham* (1856) and *The Doomed Ship* (1864). In 1865, Hazel was set to work plagiarising the story of Sweeney Todd, which Long issued in the autumn of that same year as *Sweeney Todd; or, The Ruffian Barber* followed by the strap-hanger, 'A tale of the terrors of the seas and the mysteries of the city.' It was, as even a cursory glance at one of the few surviving copies in the Indiana University Collection of Nineteenth Century Fiction reveals, an almost line-for-line theft of the Lloyd original. Whether Lloyd was ever aware of this piracy – or even particularly cared being so adept at property theft himself – there is no record.

The Harry Hazel version of the story consisted of 36 chapters and ran to 110 pages with a single engraving portraying a rather benign Sweeney Todd about to send his lather boy on a mission before getting ready to 'polish off' another victim. The title page spares any embarrassment Hazel might have felt about his appropriation by naming the author as 'Captain Merry.' Bibliographer Helen Smith has seized upon this fact in her argument that James Malcolm Rymer was the author of the original story by pointing out that 'Merry' is an anagram of Rymer.

The next version of the legend followed the chance discovery of an old copy of the Lloyd serial in a second-hand bookseller's shop in London in 1878. The buyer happened to be a member of the staff of another astute publisher, Charles Fox, who ran a small empire of penny bloods and magazines in Shoe Lane just off Fleet Street. It seems probable that Fox was familiar with the events that had occurred around the corner from his office and their enduring nature presented an opportunity for a successful addition to his list. He gave one of his writers the dog-eared copy with orders to create a much longer, 48-part version that would be sold in 24-page penny weekly editions, profusely illustrated.

Fox took the decision to advertise the story in his other publications, with a gimmick to catch the interest of readers by offering a 'Free Splendid Coloured Plate' with the first two issues. Unbeknown to Charles Fox, however, his *Sweeney Todd, The Demon Barber,* would generate a libel action by a man who was accused of being author. The serial was also responsible for some unhappy repercussions in the barbering profession.

The elements of violence, bloodshed and cannibalism in the Fox version were emphasised from the very start, with Sweeney Todd depicted as a crop-headed, bow-legged, evil-looking character. The narrative gave him the additional characteristics of lecher and violent bully. Mrs Lovett, too, was markedly less attractive, hating and distrusting Todd, and finding consolation from her unenviable task of turning corpses into meat pies, in the arms of a lover, Major Bounce. The cashiered soldier is similarly revealed in time as a confidence trickster.

Comparing the story with the Lloyd original, the first 28 episodes bear a remarkable similarity. But after Todd has been caught and thrown into Newgate, he gets a new lease of life by escaping from the prison with a new character, Reverend Joseph Lupin. The clergyman proves to be drunken philanderer who conceals his criminal tendencies under the guise of religious fervour. On the run, the ill-matched pair plot their revenge on those in society who they believe have wronged them. In an interesting episode while they are staying disguised at an inn on Hampstead Heath, a comment from the unsuspecting landlord inflates Todd's already considerable ego:

'I have just, gentlemen, been buying a portrait of the execrable Sweeney Todd and if either of you have happened to see him in London, perhaps you can tell me if it is at all like the villain. We frighten our children now, if they misbehave themselves at all, by telling them that Sweeney Todd is coming to make them into pies and then they are as quiet as possible.'

Inevitably, Sweeney Todd grows tired of his companion and cold-bloodedly murders him on the Heath before returning to his old haunts in Fleet Street. Here he manages to recover some of his hidden wealth and after setting fire to the barber shop, moves around London like a wraith, robbing unsuspecting victims and cutting throats – always keeping one step ahead of the law. Gradually, though, the net starts to close around Sweeney Todd and he attempts to flee across the Channel to France.

This time, though, there is to be no escape for the Demon Barber and he is cornered and arrested at a small village, Brighthelmstone on the South Downs. The final episode of the story is taken up with a graphic description of Todd's execution: not at Newgate but on the gallows at Tyburn. Enormous crowds turn out to watch and effigies of him are seen hanging from barber's poles all along the route bearing the words, 'Easy shaving for a penny – as good as you will find any.' The author re-emphasises the basic truth of the story, admits that the buildings and houses in Fleet Street have been changed and rebuilt since the events took place, and concludes:

'People began to be in error as to the exact spot where Sweeney Todd's shop really stood and as the year's went on the villain's name became spoken of merely as a legendary person. But he lived, as the *Newgate Calendar* of the time testifies. There is also a full-length portrait still in existence, depicting him in his shop with his old wig blocks and racks of razors.'

Not long after the appearance of the Fox version, a debate flared up as to *who* the author might be. An early favourite was Edmund Faucit Saville, an actor who was known to supplement his periods 'resting' by writing Penny Dreadfuls. Historian Walter George Bell comments on this attribution in his book *Fleet Street in Seven Centuries* (1912):

'The authorship was persistently attributed to Saville, now a distant memory of old playgoers; the best smuggler bold and pirate king and heroic naval officer that ever trod the melodramatic stage. He had a gift in composition as well as in the portrayal of character parts. Of many dramas that came from his pen, *The Murder in the Old Smithy* – a classic of its day – is best remembered. That was a play with bone in it; not the thin strand of sentiment beaten out over three hours which serves for this anaemic generation of players.'

Strong as the case for Edmund Saville might seem, the name of George Augustus Sala (1828-1895) was an even more fancied candidate. Sala was a journalist and novelist who was known to have begun his working life as an illustrator for Edward Lloyd. By his own admission, he had written items for several of the sensational publishers before embarking on a distinguished literary career. Sala became a contributor to several of the most important journals of the day, notably Dickens' *Household Words* and *The Illustrated London News*. Later he founded the *Temple Bar Magazine* – the title of which was thought to be significant by some people – and finally became a special correspondent for *The Daily Telegraph* in Europe, Russia, America and Australia.

But it was the mystery that surrounded George Sala's early penurious days – which he subsequently did much to conceal – that lead to the idea he had written the story of Sweeney Todd. James Hain Friswell, a high-minded writer on educational and semi-religious topics, first made the allegation. In a devastating attack on cheap literature *in Modern Men of Letters Honestly Criticised* published in 1870, he wrote of Sala:

'It is whispered that he wrote at one time for the excelling Mr Lloyd certain romances such as *Ada, the Betrayed, Julia, the Deserted* and the like. These penny romances were not vicious, though morbidly exciting. One called *Sweeney Todd; or, The String of Pearls* related how a certain barber in Fleet Street cut the throats of his customers and then sank them down a trap to the kitchen where they were made into, and whence they issued, as mutton-pies!'

The reference – it is obvious from the date of Friswell's accusation – is to the *original* Lloyd version. Yet subsequent writers – notably Montague Summers who observed, 'George Sala is often (and not without good reason) supposed to have been the pen employed' – have taken Friswell's reference to mean the later Fox version without checking that it appeared *seven years* after Lloyd's serial. With a little more research, these same writers might also have discovered that Sala rebuffed the allegation in the strongest possible manner in 1871 by taking Friswell to court and winning considerable damages for libel.

The hearing at the Guildhall on 17 February 1871 was widely reported and Sala defended himself fiercely against the attack of Friswell's defence counsel that he was 'a tipsy writer,' unreliable as far as publishers were concerned, and constantly on the verge of debt and imprisonment. And as to writing penny romances for Mr Lloyd, he thundered, there was not a scrap of evidence to connect him.

The case against Friswell was found proved and Sala was awarded the not inconsiderably sum for those days of £500 – with an order that copies of *Modern Men of Letters Honestly Criticised* be withdrawn from circulation. The journalist must have hoped that the record was now straight and certainly no one repeated the attribution again during his lifetime. But old libels, particularly those associated with such a notorious subject as Sweeney Todd, have a habit of reappearing. By the turn of the century the claim was being repeated at will with no one getting any closer to unmasking the real author.

In my opinion, the answer is simple: the Fox serial was written by one of his regular writers. In this case a rather elusive figure named George Savage who is believed to have taken his pen name from the famous London club which he frequented and where he picked up commissions from publishers like Lloyd, Fox and William Grant who issued his most famous novel, *The Woman with the Yellow Hair* (1865). This book, in fact, bears strong stylistic similarities to the Fox version – and Savage was known to be a man fascinated by London criminal history.

Another facet of the Sala libel case was that it promoted attacks in the press about 'the literature of rascaldom' – as a writer in the influential *Quarterly Review* for July 1890 called the flood of penny fiction then on sale everywhere. Apart from being accused of 'peopling our prisons, our reformatories and our Colonies with scapegraces and ne'er do wells,' publications such as *Sweeney Todd, the Demon Barber of Fleet Street* 'had a terrible effect on the young,' said the writer:

'When it is remembered that this foul and filthy trash circulates by the thousands and tens of thousands each week amongst the lads who are at a most impressionable period of their lives, and whom the modern system of purely secular education has left without ballast or guidance, it is not surprising that the authorities have to lament the prevalence of juvenile crime and that the Lord Mayor and Aldermen should constantly have to adjudicate in cases for which these books are directly responsible.'

However, if some critics felt the youth of Britain might be in peril by reading stories about the likes of Sweeney Todd, then the barbering profession was certainly suffering as a result of his notoriety. In a leading article about the era, which appeared in *The Times* in March 1941, the anonymous leader writer stated:

'People sacrificed almost everything to be genteel then. Sweeney Todd both on stage and in print was considered so vulgar than the word "barber" was considered vulgar, too. An old-fashioned schoolmaster once commanded his boys never, never to use such a word and always says, "hairdresser."'

The late E.S. Turner took the point up further in his admirable study of juvenile literature, *Boys Will Be Boys* (1948) claiming that the word 'hairdresser' was now used almost exclusively, 'because it was the astonishing popularity of the Sweeney Todd legend that caused a good old English word to lapse into disrepute among respectable people.'

Despite the tirades against allowing the story of Sweeney Todd to fall into the hands of juvenile readers, within a decade two publishers had issued specially abridged editions targeted at the young. The first of these was A.Ritchie & Co based in Red Lion Court who specialised in tales of young heroes such as *Union Jack: The British Boy Sailor* (1870), *The Street Waif (1876)* and *The Days of Young Jack Sheppard* (1885) as well as issuing high-sounding weekly periodicals like *The Champion Journal for the Boys of the United Kingdom.* Significantly, Ritchie also issued *The History of Newgate: A Record of the Most Celebrated Trials* and *The New Newgate Calendar: Containing a Complete History of the Remarkable Lives and Trials of Notorious Criminals Past and Present* "graphically illustrated." In 1881, the firm published *Sweeney Todd, The Barber of Fleet Street* 'A Thrilling Story of the Old City of London' with a bold sub-heading: 'Founded on Facts.' The 16-page, tabloid sized abridgement was almost certainly the work of Ritchie's busiest author, Henry Emmett, who was the editor of *The Champion Journal* and maybe for this reason toned down the violence and gore for his younger audience.

Charles Fox, too, continued to sell single volumes of the George Savage novel – 'over 150,000 copies sold' he was boasting – when on Saturday, 6 June 1885 he ran the first of six instalments of 'The String of Pearls; or, Passages from the Life of Sweeney Todd, the Demon Barber' in one of his stable of juvenile weeklies, *The Boy's Standard.* The story was an even more sanitized version of the best-seller by the magazine's editor, Philander Jackson (the pseudonym of Alfred Burrage, another hugely prolific writer who had started writing professionally at the age of fifteen) yet once again the opening paragraph made a particular point about its authenticity:

'Of all the tales of crime and bloodshed which it has fallen to the lot of the historian or novelist to chronicle, we doubt if any other can compare on the point of horror with the story of Sweeney Todd, usually called the Demon Barber of Fleet Street. This bloodthirsty wretch "flourished" if such a term may be used with regard to such a villain, during many years of the last century until at last an end was made to his career of crime, fitting in horror well with the means by which he had striven to satisfy his avarice and cupidity. Most of our readers have heard a little of how in his little shop near Temple Bar this human ghoul was in the habit of 'polishing off' any victims presumably possessed of valuables who might present themselves at his shop for a shave or what-not.'

The 'what-not' for which Sweeney Todd had been responsible was, though, by no means over and as the century drew to a close, his influence was being extended in new versions of the story published on both sides of the Atlantic.

* * *

The first writer to introduce Sweeney Todd as a secondary character in a story was Vane St John (1833-1887) another prodigious author of stories for boys who contributed to a number of the publishers of fiction and was for a time the editor of *Young Men of Great Britain.* He was the younger brother of the better known, Percy St John (1821-1889) author of one of the most famous serials of the Victorian era, *The Blue Dwarf,* who apparently introduced him to the sweat-shop labour of writing for Fox and the other publishers around Fleet Street. After producing a succession of stories with Irish settings, Vane St John had his biggest success when he introduced the Demon Barber into a serial, *The Link Boy of Old London,* which ran for 45 chapters in *The Boy's Standard,* starting on 4 November 1882. Whether Todd was introduced by the author's design or at the suggestion of Charles Fox – who was, of course, well aware of the character's appeal – is not known.

Tom is the 'Link Boy' of the title and it is through his courage and bravery that the cause of several mysterious deaths in London are traced to the Demon Barber, who has miraculously returned to the city and is now enriching himself with unsuspecting victims. Todd has changed somewhat in the interim: he is now a 'short, stout man with as round head and shaggy red hair.' His face is a mask 'of low and brutal passions' and his eyes, which are set close together against the bridge of his nose, 'give a peculiar vindictiveness to his expression.' The Demon Barber's *modus operandi* has changed somewhat, too. He has two villainous assistants who help him entrap, 'fine, plump, wealthy men' and drop them through a trap door onto a row of iron spikes. Todd has another female compatriot in the unappealing form of Mrs Darkman. In Vane St John's tale it is not the Bow Street Runners who bring him to justice, but the intrepid Tom. *The Link Boy of Old London* was reprinted several times in serial and penny-part form, but the unfortunate author soon joined the ranks of many of his fellow hacks, 'living carelessly and dying penniless,' to quote W.O.G. Lofts and D.J Adley in their *The Man Behind Boys' Fiction* (1970).

'Devlin the Barber' who appeared in a novel of that title in 1888 was Sweeney Todd in all but name. Created by Benjamin Leopold Farjeon (1833-1903), a Londoner who had worked in New Zealand for a number of years before returning to England to pursue a career as a novelist and playwright, Devlin found a ready public. Farjeon predominantly wrote mysteries, often solved by newspaper reporters who had an interest in crime much like himself. Among his most popular thrillers were *Great Porter Square* (1885), *The Mystery of Mr Fetix* (1890) and *Samuel Boyd of Catchpole Square* (1899). *Devlin the Barber,* which Farjeon's publishers, Ward & Downey issued in 1888, has been described by Chris Steinbruner and Otto Penzler in *The Encyclopaedia of Mystery and Detection* (1976) as 'perhaps the scarcest Farjeon mystery novel.'

The book's cover with the barber Devlin grinning fiendishly and brandishing a razor gave a clear indication of the contents. According to Farjeon's introduction the story was about 'a fearful mystery with which not only all London but all England is ringing,' centred on a barber's shop in Chapel Street, Westminster. Devlin, he said, was 'a peculiar name – and everything about him is that and worse.' Yet, the barber's very existence was 'doubted by some, though he did live and among us.' Farjeon's familiarity with the Sweeney Todd legend is again in evidence when he adds:

'He kept a saloon, as I dare say you remember hearing of; shaving three pence, hair cutting four pence. He had a wax lady's head in the window almost like flesh and blood that went around by machinery. It brought him customers from all over London.'

Devlin apparently caters to female customers, 'and what's more has a private room set apart to do 'em up in.' Women, it seems, are enchanted by the tall, dark man with his black moustache, curling at the ends, although he has a laugh that makes people's hair stand on end: 'It wasn't the laugh of a human creature; there was something unearthly about it,' Farjeon says. And he quotes one customer as saying, 'While he was bending over me, he was like one of them vampires you read about.'

When the bodies of several customers who believed to have visited Devlin are found murdered, suspicion naturally focuses on him. The narrator then manages to get himself into the barber's premises in the hope of being able expose the killer. On his first night, though, the young man has a terrible dream in which he imagines having his brain cut out by a razor. In the morning he is in for an even bigger surprise when Devil tells him that *he* knows the identity of the killer. In a cleverly handled finale, Farjeon turns the reader's suspicions completely around by revealing the barber is actually a private investigator who has set up in the profession to catch the real murderer: a debauched nobleman who selects his victims from customers at barber shops where he can observe them without attracting attention.

There was to be no such deception in the story of a French barber, Barnabe Cabard, his female accomplice and a third murderer who assists the pair in *L'Auberge des trios rois (The Inn of the Three Kings)* a mammoth tale of 1290 pages by Jules Beaujoint, published by Artheme Fayard in 1890. Beaujoint was one of half a dozen pen-names of prolific local writer, Jean Vaucheret (1830-1893), who wrote a series of imaginative crime stories published in *livraisons* of eight-pages, notably *L 'auberge aux tueurs, Les descendants de Leblanc* and *L'auberge sanglantede Peirebeilhe* based on a famous true murder story which inspired many later crime writers and was the basis for a classic 1951 movie, *L'auberge rouge (The Red Inn),* starring Ferndandel, Julian Carette and Francoise Rosay.

The setting for the story of the murderous Cabard is the Rue des Marmousets in Paris in the 1770s and the similarities between him and Sweeney Todd are not difficult to spot from the beginning of the *livraisaon* – except that the Frenchman doubles as pie maker to dispose of his victims. It is quite probable, of course, that Jules Beaujoint was familiar with the French tradition of murderous barbers. I have already mentioned the 400-year-old ballad *of Le jeuene homme empoisonne* (The Young Man Who Was Poisoned) and the Eighteenth Century tale of the 'Demon Barber of the Rue de la Harpe,' which had been familiar to readers for generations.

Beaujoint does not spare the blood and gore. Chapter after chapter recounts the cunning schemes of *Cabard – Perruquier* as he inveigles customers into his shop and then unceremoniously slays them. The bodies are dumped into the cellar below and swiftly butchered for sale as pies in the *Patissiere* of his accomplice, Pierre Moullon, next door. These 'delicacies' are held in high regard by the local gentry and whenever stocks run low, Cabard calls on Moullon to help lure more male – and occasionally female – victims to a similar fate. Just like his London counterpart, Bamabe Cabard has to survive a number of narrow escapes until the suspicions of a young man who unwittingly falls in love with the other conspirator, Cabard's female assistant, finally leads to his arrest and execution.

The gruesome illustrations accompanying Beaujoint's story continued the tradition that had begun in the original 'Penny Dreadful' and evidently delighted French readers as much as the original 'fierce' engravings. Then, with the emergence of comic strips for children, Sweeney Todd enjoyed a new burst of popularity. A few typical examples will have to suffice for many more.

Jasper Todd was the central character in 'The Inn of a Thousand Secrets' which ran in *The Bullseye* from the autumn of 1932 to 1933. A grasping little man with red hair, glinting eyes, twitching fingers and a throaty chuckle, he is the ungenial host of the isolated Red Fox Inn which rarely has customers – for long. In the cobwebbed bar stands a massive chair, beautifully carved, with a padded leather seat and arm rests. It is clearly Todd's pride and joy and during the course of the series is used to dump unsuspecting customers into an underground cavern where they are imprisoned and robbed. The saga featured all manner of victims from a one-legged sailor on the run from the law to a pretty young girl motorist whose car breaks down near the inn – all of whom fall into the demon innkeeper's trap. Finally, it was his fate to be dispatched in his own his fiendish device.

A very eye-catching illustration enhanced the cover of a 110-page paperback version of the story published in 1936 by C. Arthur Pearson of London in their six-penny 'True Crimes Series.' No author was named for *Sweeney Todd The Demon Barber,* but it may well have been the handiwork of one of the company's female writers, Marie C. Leighton, who specialised in mystery stories. Certainly this is the most genteel version of the story to date, with Mrs Lovett presented as

Todd's foolish wife, a meek and confused woman completely in his power who finally takes her own life. The tale itself ends:

'It was never made clear how Todd got rid of the bodies of his various victims, the men who he had murdered and robbed. There was one horrible rumour which grew into a legend in the neighbourhood that Mrs Lovett's pie shop had disposed of them, but such a thing is too horrible to contemplate.'

There were no such reservations from either the author or publishers when the shadow of Sweeney Todd returned again to the bookstalls after the Second World War. Amidst the welter of gaudy pulp paperbacks which clamoured for readers in 1953 was *Demon Barber of Broadway* complete with a sub-heading, 'There was a Sweeney Todd in New York, too' and a bosomy young beauty dumbstruck as a man in a barber's chair is about to have his throat slit. The publishers of this ephemeral two shilling book were Modern Fiction of Morwell Street, run by E.H. Turvey, another entrepreneur in the Edward Lloyd tradition, while the author, 'Griff,' a man not unlike so many of the hacks before him who had kept the legend alive. The blurb on the back of the book outlined the story: again reminding readers of the original Demon Barber:

'In this thrilling counterpart of the Sweeney Todd story, Griff tells of a similar killer on the Bronx end of New York's Broadway and introduces for the first time the Herculean private eye, Rapier Codd, known as "Swordfish" and his glamorous, exotic Polish girlfriend, Ilma Podoki, who tangled with him in gangland. "Swordfish" carries his life in his hands and his tackling of the "demon barber" problem is so brilliantly described that you fancy you are there . . .'

The terse, action-packed style of *Demon Barber of Broadway* might well have been the handiwork of a modern day Thomas Prest and it has similarly taken some years to discover the true identity of the author. Once again, 'Griffs' knowledge of the Sweeney Todd story is evident, and he utilises this in the story of a gang of diamond robbers who are using a barbershop at the Bronx end of Broadway near the Harlem River as a "front" for murdering their victims. Tracking down one of the gang to the premises, Codd is an eyewitness to a scene that might easily have occurred in Fleet Street, 150 years earlier:

'He hadn't been there long before he saw in the streetlights the familiar ungainly figure of Kalong who seemed to have been drinking.

He lurched against the sides of the passage as he went in the barbershop. Swordfish figured that Kalong was going for a shave on account of going somewhere special that evening. He resolved to tail him wherever he went. But ten minutes went by – a quarter of an hour – half an hour: and there wasn't any sign of Kalong coming out.'

The private eye and his girl friend take turns to watch the shop, but it is Ilma who sees their worst fears confirmed when a thunderstorm suddenly causes the roller blind in the front window of the shop to fly up:

'Instantly the oblong of the window shone brilliantly, save where two shadows stood vividly etched on the glass. One shadow showed the profile of a man's head, tilted upwards as it lay on the backrest of the barbering chair. The other shadow showed a hand, part of an arm, and the blade of a razor. The razor swept down and across, merged completely into the shadowed throat, the head started up and forward, only to be covered and dragged back by a shapeless mass of black. Ilma's mouth sagged open. She felt like fainting. She had seen the shadowgraph of a man's throat being cut and his head enveloped in a towel directly the fatal steel had done its work.'

Griff brings the drama of the *Demon Barber of Broadway* to a surprise conclusion. On the final page, Ilma's father, a man driven mad by the underworld of New York, is revealed as the barber and consigned to an institution.

Researcher W.O.G. Lofts who investigated many of the aspects of the Sweeney Todd legend during his lifetime, was convinced the man behind the pen name was Ernest McKeag (1896-1974) an editor with the Amalgamated Press who also moonlighted producing gangster novels for publishers like Modern Fiction. Lofts' reasons are convincing. McKeag had begun his career working for Lloyds Newspapers Ltd – the company that had evolved from Edward Lloyd's 'Penny Dreadful' empire – but after they had collapsed in 1922 began writing juvenile fiction, detective tales and various 'sensational novels.' After war service with the Royal Navy, McKeag's versatility enabled him to quickly find work again.

McKeag lived in a flat in Chancery Lane and – according to Lofts – often walked through Fleet Street on his way to work at Amalgamated Press. He was familiar with the Sweeney Todd legend and was never slow at making use of ideas easily to hand. He was also an enthusiast of amateur dramatics and may well have appeared in a version of Sweeney Todd staged by the Fleetway Players in the early Fifties. It is, however, Ernest McKeag's literary style that has caused the doubts about his authorship of this particular story. Another researcher, Steve Holland, has carefully compared the style of the *Demon Barber of Broadway* with the work of another prolific author of the period – as well as the records of Modern Fiction Publishing – and is convinced the credit belongs to Frank Dubrez Fawcett (1891-1968). Holland has established that McKeag only wrote five of the 'Griff' novels and the story of the American demon barber was not one of them.

Fawcett was a former newspaper reporter and advertising copywriter who had begun writing risque novels of bohemian life in the Thirties such as *Shop Soiled* and *A Bride from the Street,* augmented by series like 'World's Strangest Stories' and true crime stories for London newspapers and magazines. The success of the 'Hard Boiled' English writers, Peter Cheyney and James Hadley Chase, inspired Fawcett to create the seductive Mabbie Otis whose violent adventures among the low life of London started with *Miss Otis Comes to Piccadilly* (1946) and went on to sell over five million copies. But Fawcett, whose identity was hidden behind the pen name Ben Sarto, was only paid a flat-fee for each book and had to take on other work, as Steve Holland has explained:

'At his peak, Fawcett was writing a book every two weeks, straight into his typewriter without even a read-through until he got the printer's proofs. His gutter-slang style that owed nothing to American idiom and everything to his imagination quickly drew in his readers and his characters were drawn in confident strokes of his pen. He was responsible for hundreds of cheap paperbacks titles and wrote most of the "Griff" titles for Modern Fiction. There is no doubt that *Demon of Broadway* is his work.'

If there is any further doubt, Holland has pointed out that Fawcett was making a special study of Charles Dickens' London the year before publication of his version of the Sweeney Todd legend. He had also done some amateur dramatics in Dickensian plays and lectured on the author. His study, *Dickens the Dramatist,* published in 1952, is a valuable source of information – though it gives no hint that the man who wrote it was also the creator of gaudy paperbacks like the *Demon Barber of Broadway.*

Apart from the cheap paperbacks, several comic book publishers around this time also saw the potential of the Sweeney Todd legend. C. Arthur Pearson, who had already exploited him in a novel, obviously felt there was something that might appeal to readers of comics. No sign of slashing razors, though, or flesh-filled pies. The result was the first appearance in comic strip form of 'Sweeney Tod' – the final 'd' was deliberately dropped – in *The Monster Comic* in 1939. Drawn by the versatile Hugh McNeill, the barber had a gormless assistant, 'Lathering Leonard' who more often than not thwarted his boss's fiendish, but futile schemes.

In 1950, the popular boy's comic, *Rover,* again transferred Todd across the Atlantic as 'The Demon Barber of the Six Trails" in which he was actually on the side of the law and lured the bad guys into his shop before dropping them into ready made cells below. This would appear to be the only time that the revolving chair has been used for good reasons! A quarter of a century later, in 1977, one of the great comic illustrators of his generation, Leo Baxendale, creator of the immortal Bash Street Kids, gave young readers of *Whoopee!* young 'Sweeney Toddler,' a violent infant whose exploits terrorising everyone including his long suffering mother became so popular that he later moved to the comic's front page.

Yet another new medium welcomed Sweeney Todd in 1992, when one of the leading modern horror story writers, Neil Gaiman (1960-) creator of the best-selling *Sandman* series (1989-1996), came up with the idea for a graphic novel, *Sweeney Todd – Penny Dreadful,* in partnership with the American artist, Michael Zulli. Using a mixture of old engravings, prints, photographs and new artwork, the pair produced a groundbreaking visual work that examined the fact and fiction behind the character. Gaiman explained his inspiration in an interview with Steve Bissette *of Comic Buyer's Guide* in July 1992:

'When Mike and I were together one day it became apparent that both of us were fascinated by Stephen Sondheim's *Sweeney Todd.* We talked about Sweeney and I said that he goes back much further than the musical and we should do something about him. We flew over to London and took a grand tour of Fleet Street. Both of us are research junkies and the resulting story is very research-heavy.'

Gaiman knew that the original version of the story had been published in 'Penny Dreadful' format and was keen to go full-circle and publish this latest version in instalments in a magazine, *Taboo,* before going into book format. His research also threw up a fascinating new aspect of the Sweeney Todd legend.

'Do you know the place where Sweeney Todd was killing people is one of the boundaries of London? When the reigning monarch reaches Temple Bar, they have to dismount and perform a ritual with a pearl-handled razor – actually a pearl-handled sword – before entering the city? The original title for the story was *The String of Pearls,* so if the reigning monarch has to dismount at Temple Bar and perform a ritual with a pearl-handled blade, I think you are talking about things that recur. The place where Sweeney was killing people is one of the boundaries of London. Could we be looking at what is essentially a sacrificial act? That Sweeney and Mrs Lovett are inherited roles? Isn't it possible that people may *still* be doing it?'

Neil Gaiman has no doubt that the tale of Sweeney Todd is one of the most intriguing of all legends and certain to endure. He says of his version and its place in this tradition: 'The mystique of Sweeney is the magic of the past as a series of reflecting and distorting mirrors that satisfy different needs.'

Neil Gaiman's modern version of Sweeney Todd.

18

'Attend The Tale of Sweeney Todd'

One of the most intriguing pieces of evidence that came to light during my search for the origins of Sweeney Todd was an item from a theatre not unlike those where the story of the Demon Barber has been performed for a century and a half since George Dibdin Pitt's *The String of Pearls* made its debut in March 1847. Curious as this may seem — curiouser still is the fact the theatre was not in London, but America: The Frazee on 42nd Street in New York City. In this unpretentious little playhouse, located just to the west of that famous street of theatres, Broadway, a melodrama entitled *Todd* opened on 1 September 1924. How the theatre came to put on this production, its claim for the authenticity of the story, and the play's subsequent influence on dramatised versions is a tale almost as unusual as the man who gave his name to the theatre.

Harry Frazee (1881-1929) was a theatrical producer, best remembered today for mounting the hit musical, *No, No Nanette* in 1925 with those famous songs, 'Tea for Two' and 'I Want To Be Happy.' Frazee was also the owner of the well-known baseball team, the Boston Red Sox, who won the 1918 World Series. Not long after this triumph, Frazee sold the star player, the legendary Babe Ruth, to his friend, Colonel Jacob Ruppert, owner of their greatest rivals, the New York Yankees. Although the Red Sox subsequently played in three World Series, they never won another game — and many Bostonians believed there was a curse on the team because of Harry Frazee's act of baseball heresy.

The Frazee Theatre did not fare much better, either, and *Todd* became one of the sixty short run plays performed during the pre-war years before its doors were closed forever. The building no longer exists today and for many years there was no trace of any records documenting its history. Indeed, the information about the Frazee's version of the Demon Barber story might also have disappeared if some theatrical accounts, copies of the plays and boxes of sheet music had not been discovered by an antique collector, Vivian Cord, in 1972 and given to the University of Texas. Among this collection of memorabilia was a faded copy of the programme for *Todd* containing the note that instantly caught my attention. It read:

'The play of *Todd* is based on the life of an actual character of the same name; an account appeared in *The Newgate Calendar* dated 29 January 1802. Here are the brief details of the main points: "In all our Annals of crime, no blacker-hearted villain than Sweeney Todd ever existed. He met his doom on Tuesday morning last at 8 o'clock. John Ketch officiated in his usual role as Hangman. To the last Todd remained defiant, he refused all spiritual aid and consolation and died with a curse on his lips. His body was cut down and buried in quicklime within the prison-walls. Todd was born at Stepney in London, October 26, 1756. In his early life he was apprenticed to a cutter, but being accused by his employer, a Mr Wilberforce, of a petty theft he was condemned to a sentence of five years hard labour. He protested in vain his innocence. Upon his release his nature became so hardened and embittered that he swore a perpetual vengeance against the human race."'

The sentence in this that particularly caught my eye was the suggestion of Sweeney Todd being driven by vengeance to redress the wrong done to him. In fact, this has become a persistent theme in versions of the legend ever since that 1924 production and, in particular, the magnificent Stephen Sondheim musical and a recent trio of television productions. It is interesting to discover how this has happened in the words of those responsible for transforming the traditionally evil figure of repertory theatre into a troubled man driven by terrible circumstances beyond his control.

A good deal of the credit for this change of character belongs to the English playwright Christopher Bond (1948-) who was unexpectedly forced into a creating a new version in 1974 when, by his reckoning, there had been at least six different adaptations of George Dibdin Pitt's original. He explained the background to this landmark moment in an article for *The Guardian* in June 1980:

'I was working as an actor at the Victorian Theatre, Stoke-on-Trent and volunteered to write the play to get us off the hook. We'd announced that we were doing *Sweeney Todd* and then the Artistic Director, Peter Cheeseman, and Ron Daniels, who was going to direct it, decided they didn't like any of the extant versions.'

Bond says that he and the two partners had come to the conclusion that all these versions were very thin on plot, in the characters on stage and a dialogue that was accessible to modern audiences:

'My first concern in writing a new version was to tell an exciting story that involved the audience with its characters. So I started off by writing an outline that spliced elements of Dumas' *The Count of Monte Cristo* and Tourneur's *The Revenger's Tragedy* around the central images of a barber who cuts throats and a neighbour who turns the bodies into pies. Next I added a romantic subplot based loosely around *Twelfth Night* and *Pericles* in which the traditional male/female roles were somewhat reversed – but the *Pericles* didn't fit in the end because it held up the action and had to go. I then threw in chunks of market patter and wise saws and modern instances from Brenda my greengrocer and began writing in earnest.'

Christopher Bond went to considerable trouble to build up the more sensational aspects of the story – the throat cutting, revolving chair and meat pies – and carefully plot the eight murders seen on stage so that each would have a separate impact on the audience. Much to his surprise, he says, the piece almost wrote itself and he was very pleased with the eventual production. But the next phase in the life of his new adaptation was to provide Bond with an even bigger surprise:

'Since then, *Sweeney Todd* has been performed all over the place, including the Theatre Royal, Stratford East, where Stephen Sondheim saw it, liked it, and contacted me to ask if I'd agree to his using it as the basis for a musical. I agreed. His original idea was to turn it into a 'ballad opera' all singing and no dialogue, but although this eventually proved impracticable, there is still only a minimal amount of dialogue and the plot line is largely carried by Sondheim's ingenious lyrics. What I like most about the show is that while the plot, characters and spirit of the original have survived, the music has supercharged it.'

Of course, Stephen Sondheim (1930-) brought a wealth of experience and an impressive list of credits to the challenge of setting the story of the Demon Barber to music. Originally inspired by the lyricist Oscar Hammerstein II, Sondheim had already written the lyrics to a string of Broadway hits including *West Side Story* (1957), *Gypsy* (1959) *A Funny Thing Happened on the Way to the Forum* (1962) and *A Little Night Music* (1973). Nonetheless, the story of the return of Sweeney Todd to London after 15 years transportation to Australia on a trumped up charge and his quest for vengeance on the lecherous judge who had seduced his beautiful wife and wrecked his life, called upon all Sondheim's skills – not the least the requirement for 25 songs. From the first time he had seen Christopher Bond's adaptation, he said he had a clear vision of the Demon Barber as a man who 'hears the music no one else can hear.' As the lyricist later put it in an interview with *The Times:* 'You've got a villain who does it for the money and a murderer who does it for love.'

Todd was visualised as a love-torn killer and Mrs Lovett, a cheery East Ender churning up the bones in her mincer for the pies. However, the show had problems in rehearsals and preview – the audiences being either unresponsive or shocked, according to Sondheim – and also required 271 investors to provide the $900,000 required for capitalisation: a record number for a Broadway show. *Sweeney Todd: The Demon Barber of Fleet Street,* 'A Musical Thriller' finally opened on 1 March, 1979 at the Uris Theatre to excellent reviews, with praise for the songs, Hal Prince's direction and the co-stars, Len Cariou and Angela Lansbury. *Time* magazine lead the applause.

'As Sweeney, Cariou performs with epic ashen gravity like a scion of the House of Usher summoned forth by Poe. Quite wonderful and totally different is Lansbury's Mrs Lovett, a blowsy pragmatist as wickedly succulent as one of her pies. Within a broodingly ominous set, Harold Prince directs his accomplished forces with the flash, flourish and panache of a Broadway Patton.'

Those American critics who suggested the musical might be in for a long ran could not have been proved more right when, the following year, it transferred to London. There it was staged at The Theatre Royal, Drury Lane, heralded as 'Britain's most expensive musical ever' (at £500,000) with Denis Quilley and Sheila Hancock in the leading roles. Such was the interest in this programme that London Weekend Television devoted their prestigious *South Bank Show* to the mounting of the show and a review of the legend of Sweeney Todd. Much of my original research material was embodied into the programme hosted by Melvyn Bragg.

What I personally found most satisfying at the opening night in London was its attempt to recreate the locality in which the Demon Barber had lived. Indeed, looking at the complex scenery of decaying buildings, iron structures and sulphurous smoking chimneys was almost like a case of *deja vu* for me – reminding me of what I had seen in my mind's eye all those years before when I had first started to research the life of Sweeney Todd. *The Times* critic, Irving Wardle, put this feeling into words in his review the following morning:

'London is presented as a vision of hell people with ragged madwomen, asylum directors, corrupt officials and a populace gorging themselves on the tasty dishes that Sweeney Todd and Mrs Lovett make. The show rivets you to your seat, freezes your blood, and leaves you with the feeling that the Demon Barber is alive and well and sitting all around you in Drury Lane.'

For some other critics, like Robert Cushman of *The Observer*, 'the show touched greatness' and he saw echoes from past versions of the story when audiences had 'listened raptly and cheered at the end.' Michael Billington in *The Guardian* added his own praise – along with another striking example of presentiment:

'There is no doubt that Sondheim and Prince have conceived a remarkable Brechtian barber's opera and totally transformed an antique melodrama. It is a brilliant piece of musical theatre; a dense, complex, thorough-composed work that would not have disgraced – indeed would have enhanced – the stages of opera houses throughout the world. I am convinced that, like most of Stephen Sondheim's work, it will have a life beyond its immediate run.'

Indeed it has. As I write these words, the show is still playing in different parts of the world. Among the leading actors who have ensured this success have been Alan Armstrong and Julia McKenzie (1993) – with Denis Quilley reversing his role from barber to judge – Dave Willetts and Jeanette Ranger (1996) and Steven Page and Beverley Klein (2002). More recently still, the pairing of the operatic stars, Sir Thomas Allen and Felicity Palmer, supported by a 50-piece orchestra, at the Royal Opera at Covent Garden added yet another new dimension to this success story.

In July 2007, the Sondheim melodrama was 'modernised' at the Festival Hall in London with the magnificent Welsh bass-baritone, Bryn Terfel, playing Sweeney in jeans and a black shirt on a stage entirely devoid of scenery. David Freeman's unique production cleverly combined the old setting of the story with the present day in a masterful mixture of gallows humour and Grand Guignol, that prompted Richard Morrison of *The Times* to enthuse, 'there will be few sights more terrifying in the West End than that of Terfel leaping into the auditorium searching for his next hapless customer – his face locked in a psychotic leer, his voice like thunder, his razor slashing like a scythe.' The production also received acclaim for Maria Freedman's 'insanely cheerful Mrs Lovett who makes cannibalism seem almost cosy as she turns corpses into the tastiest pies in London' – in the opinion of Charles Spencer of the *Daily Telegraph* – and the young ensemble from the Guildford School of Acting who evoked a London full of potential Demon Barbers, all pulling out razors at the final curtain to slash their throats. Further confirmation – if such is required – that Sondheim's masterpiece is proving to be one of the truly great modern musicals.

Indeed, the passing years have seen the musical metamorphose into a classic of modern opera, all the time underlining the enduring theatrical appeal of the legend.

For Stephen Sondheim the triumph of his work – which seizes audiences with its very first line, 'Attend the tale of Sweeney Todd!' – could not have been keener. As he explained to *The Times* when visiting England for the opening of yet another production in 2004, 'I've been an Anglophile since my first visit here in my twenties and I wrote *Sweeney Todd* partly as a love letter to London.'

* * *

Television first homed-in on the Sweeney Todd story in 1970 when the veteran Independent Television scriptwriter, Vincent Tilsley, created *Sweeney Todd; or, The Daydreamer in the Dark* for the ABC series, *Mystery arid Imagination,* The hour-long adaptation for the long-running series concentrated on Todd's struggle with his conscience and his greed for money and influence. Freddie Jones gave a lip-smacking, eye-rolling, bloodthirsty performance as he polished off his victims and won the favours of a juicy Mrs Lovett, played by Heather Canning. In a skilfully executed special effects finale in Todd's shop, Tilsley showed the barber sitting in his chair, shaving his throat and plunging into the cellar below. Viewers were then startled to see that the tilting chair was actually an illusion and the tormented Sweeney had taken his own life.

Sky commissioned the second television production, *The Tale of Sweeney Todd* with the shout-line, 'Everything You've Feared . . . Is True' in 1998. Filmed in the back streets of Dublin and at the Ardmore Studios in Ireland, it starred leading English actors, Ben Kingsley – who received a Screen Actors Guild Best Actor nomination for his performance – and the versatile Joanna Lumley. Directed by John Schlesinger and scripted by Peter Buckman, the storyline put great emphasis on the English class system of the time and how it enabled Todd to prey on the affluent members of society and sell their jewellery with seeming impunity, making the most of prejudice and his own unique 'disposal system.'

A new character was also introduced into this version of the story: an American insurance investigator, Ben Carlyle (Campbell Scott) who is trying to track down $50,000 worth of missing diamonds. Along the way he encounters corruption wherever he turns to in London as the case leads him inexorably to Sweeney Todd's shop in Fleet Street. Reviewing the first screening on 13 April, 1998 *Variety* called the production 'a grittily stylish treatment' and continued:

'Without overstating the matter, the production places Sweeney and Lovett's murderous greed in the context of a rapacious, desperate sense of class-consciousness and aspiration on the part of many Londoners of the time. Unlike the character in Stephen Sondheim's musical, this Mrs Lovett is not a woman in love. She is, rather, Sweeney's formidable business partner, who happens to be his mistress. There's nothing resembling tenderness between these two, who tear at each other, physically and verbally, with a passionless lust. More heated is the battle of wills over the right moment to take their profit and call it a day – the hard-as-nails Lovett insists the time is now, while the far-gone Sweeney just can't let go just yet.'

The third of the trio of television adaptations, *Sweeney Todd,* with the catch-line, 'A dark tale of love, obsession, murder and ultimately redemption' was subtly and even sympathetically written by British screenwriter Joshua St Johnston. He carried out his own extensive research into the story and despite admitting that he was not completely satisfied by the evidence, told *The Independent,* 'Maybe there was a Sweeney Todd after all – he just never got caught.'

The £1.8million production was directed by David Moore and starred the redoubtable English boxer turned hard-man actor, Ray Winstone – who, by a curious coincidence, had only recently co-starred with Ben Kingsley in a gangster movie, *Sexy Beast,* co-starring with Australian actress, Essie Davis. Production costs were again given as the reason for not filming in London and an entire Fleet Street set was built in Romania at Media Pro Studios on the outskirts of Bucharest.

From the outset, this *Sweeney Todd was* to have a very specific angle, as Producer Gub Neal, famous for the crime series, *Cracker* and *Prime Suspect,* explained when BBC One screened the programme in January 2006:

'Sweeney is a product of his upbringing. He was abused as a child, betrayed by his father and thrown into Newgate Jail where he was raped and saw his brother hang. This has left him vulnerable and worthy of a quiet sympathy. A lot of his rage stems from a sense of impotence and an inability to stop bad things happening. Sweeney is a man isolated from the world. He wants to be empowered to change things, so he takes it upon himself to become an angel of vengeance.'

After his days in Newgate, Neal says, Todd has become a recluse in the world of soap, wigs and perfume that form a barrier between him and the stinking society beyond his front door. But his past comes back to haunt him, first in the form of a jailer, then his Dickensian father, drunkenly threatening blackmail. Neal expanded on this concept:

'We've given the story a modern psychological complexity, having a character who finds himself compelled to do something that he knows is wrong – but who cannot stop himself. So he is caught up in the tragedy of being aware of what this is doing to him, like Macbeth or Richard III who are driven to evil but incapable of understanding the nature of what they are bringing on themselves.'

Ray Winstone, who was born and grew up on the rough streets of Hackney, felt he was ideally suited to play a tough Londoner but it was vital not to brush out the Demon Barber's brutality:

'The minute you start to compromise, you have lost it. You go for the truth of the character and don't worry about who you're going to upset. Censoring a drama is like taking a painting by Constable and rubbing out half of it. Ours is a much darker, more compelling version. There's plenty of claret, but at its heart this is the story of a man who has plenty of problems and many of them stem from the fact that he's deeply in love with Mrs Lovett, but his past stops him from being able to love her.'

A crucial moment in the story occurs when the sadistic jailer who made the young Sweeney's life a living hell comes to his shop for a shave and the barber exacts a terrible revenge. He is driven to more killing when Mrs Lovett discovers that he is impotent and takes a series of lovers. As Sweeney's rage deepens, he packages up the flesh of his victims for her to bake into pies. When Todd is finally caught and imprisoned in Newgate, he is asked by the Magistrate Sir John Fielding why he committed his terrible murders and replies memorably, 'Because I could – and then I could not.' Like Freddie Jones in the earlier production, he slits his throat.

The reviewers almost without exception commended the production – *The Observer* declaring, 'a triumphant sort of Todd, while also being visually and aurally quite unspeakably horrible and perverse on every conceivable lever' – and Ray Winston added a final thought on his character:

'I hope we showed the human story, the reasons why he behaved as he did. I always thought Sweeney Todd was a real geezer – and no doubt there are probably plenty like him walking around today.'

An intriguing if unnerving thoughts – just like so much that surrounds the story of Sweeney Todd. What is beyond doubt now, though, is that this unique murderer who went to the gallows almost two hundred years ago has found fame far beyond that of almost any other criminal. The Demon Barber's famous catch-phrase is surely destined to ring out for many a year to come:

'Oh, how I love to polish 'em off!'

Envoi

The story of Sweeney Todd has found an even greater prominence in the history of London since I first walked down Fleet Street more than half a century ago searching for the facts of his life and violent career. The signs of this new interest are to be found both in print and in city landmarks.

After two centuries of absence, the Demon Barber at last has an entry in the *Dictionary of National Biography,* which, following several years of revision and rewriting, appeared in a new edition in September 2004. One of the editors, Colin Matthew, approached me while this mammoth reference work about the great, the good and the infamous was in preparation, with a request to write an entry on Sweeney Todd. I thought he deserved a place among the enormous diversity of men and women who have shaped English history and used the summation of my research to provide a resume of the man's life which is there for anyone to read among the 15,113 other lives crammed into sixty blue-bound volumes.

It is interesting to note, too, that where once historians dismissed Sweeney Todd as an urban myth, now even the finest modern historians like Peter Ackroyd and Roy Porter have referred to him in their works about London. Ackroyd, for example, is particularly interesting on the subjects of Fleet Street and the Bow Street Runners during the time of the Demon Barber in his mammoth work, *London: The Biography* (2000). Roy Porter, for his part, has made some significant comments in *London: A Social History* (1994), especially when he refers to the 'seedier associations' of Fleet Street;

'Particularly notorious were its clandestine "Fleet Marriages", conducted mostly by clergymen imprisoned for debt in the Fleet but allowed the "liberties of the Fleet". Though an end was put to Fleet marriages by Lord Hardwicke's Marriage Act (1753), the local shenanigans of Sweeney Todd over Joanna's nuptials suggest that the area long continued under a cloud of matrimonial ill-repute.'

Two of London's great landmarks associated with the legend have suffered very different fates recently. Temple Bar, which once lowered over Sweeney Todd's little barbershop and was then removed, to spend years in the middle of a wood in Hertfordshire was finally returned to London in November 2004. Conversely, Bow Street magistrate's court was forced to close its doors in July 2006 after almost three hundred years upholding the law. Its cases were being moved to Horseferry Road in adjacent Westminster.

The magnificent gateway of Temple Bar in fact marked the boundary between the cities of London and Westminster from 1672 until 1878 when it was unceremoniously consigned to Theobald's Park in Hertfordshire. Thought to have been the work of Christopher Wren, the stone edifice with its four magnificent statues by John Bushnell – Charles I & II, James I and Anne of Denmark – it was finally returned to London after years of campaigning by the Temple Bar Trust. Fully repaired and restored, it now stands on a new site adjoining St Paul's Cathedral. Despite the objections from some quarters that the gateway should have been returned to its original position – completely impractically considering how busy that spot adjacent to the Law Courts is nowadays – Temple Bar has become a tourist attraction again, just half a mile east from where it earned its initial fame and later notoriety from association with Sweeney Todd.

In contrast, Bow Street Magistrates Court on the edge of Covent Garden was shut down two years later after 271 years to be converted into a hotel. Since Sir John Fielding heard one of the first charges in the dock – in 1760 against the renowned womaniser, Giacomo Casanova, accused of assaulting a prostitute and 'bound over to keep the peace' – many famous and notorious public figures, have been 'put up' for judgement. Notably Oscar Wilde for 'committing indecent acts' in 1895, the suffragettes, Emmeline and Christabel Pankhurst (1908), the Nazi propagandist, William 'Lord Haw-Haw' Joyce (1945) plus an endless stream of villains from the wife-murderer, Dr Hawley Crippen (1910) to the East End gangsters, 'Mad' Frankie Fraser (1946) and the Kray twins. Ronnie and Reggie Kray (1968). All stood in the famous wrought-iron dock to answer charges before one or other of the thirty three chief magistrates to have held the post.

Appropriately, the final day in the most famous lower court in the world saw a succession of cases not unlike those that would have been heard in Sweeney Todd's day – begging, prostitution, drunkenness, petty crime (including shoplifting £200 worth of negligees from a store) and a soldier accused of taking part in a pub brawl.

Elsewhere in this country and abroad the name of Sweeney Todd continues to exert a real fascination for people. The tradition in the British Army during the Second World War to call soldiers named Todd by the nickname 'Sweeney' – and vice-versa – and to designate any improvised barber's shops with the words 'Sweeney Todd, Tobruk' (et al) has been reported again from the conflict in Iraq. Barbers who were once so anxious to avoid association with the Fleet Street killer have been hanging pictures and photographs of Todd in their premises to *attract* custom; while pubs named 'Sweeney's' and 'Sweeney & Todd' can be found in places as disparate as Sidcup and Reading.

In entertainment, too, the Demon Barber is set to reach the world stage and become an even bigger icon in this century than he has been in the past two. The Stephen Sondheim musical has been used as the basis for a major new Hollywood film, *Sweeney Todd*, directed by Tim Burton and starring Johnny Depp. The combination of these two stellar talents in yet another version of the legend followed many months of rumours before the film finally went before the cameras at Pinewood Studios in February 2007. Stories that the British director, Sam Mendes, was to direct the picture were finally quashed when DreamWorks announced that Tim Burton, one of the great modern *horrormeisters* of the cinema, was to take charge and had cast Depp in the role of Sweeney Todd.

Although Burton and Depp had a long running and successful working relationship – the actor had been the star of his *Edward Scissorhands (1990)*, *Sleepy Hollow (1999)*, *Charlie and the Chocolate Factory (2005)* and *Corpse Bride (2005)* – there were those who thought the casting seemed a bigger gamble than usual. Depp's youthfulness and his singing voice were, in particular, questioned. But those who looked deeper sensed the chemistry. There was the star's portrayal of several 'iconic loners' from his debut as Glen Lantz one of the victims in *Nightmare in Elm Street (1984)* through to the unforgettable Edward Scissorhands – a dry run for the razor-wielding Demon Barber is ever there was one.

Johnny Depp's own life-story also seemed to be leading him towards playing the Demon Barber of Fleet Street. The family name, for instance, is of French Huguenot origination – emanating from a Pierre Deppe who settled in Virginia around 1700 – and the divorce of his parents when he was a teenager, which deeply traumatised him and prompted years of self-harming. In a 1993 interview, Depp confessed: 'My body is a journal in a way. It's like what sailor's used to do, where every tattoo meant something. A specific time in your life when you make a mark on yourself – whether you do it yourself with a knife or with a professional tattoo artist.'

The script for Burton's *Sweeney Todd* was written by John Logan. But it took very few liberties with the Sondheim book, as the lyricist explained in July 2007. 'It's got a lot of blood in it and that's fine by me. Some of the music has been cut in the interests of time, but I know that trying to do the full stage text would have made the film too long. There are some cuts in the songs, and some cuts within some of the songs. But generally it is pretty much the same score. The plot is also very little changed and pretty faithful to the original.'

In preparing for the role, Depp, who had actually played a guitar since he was 12 and was briefly a rock musician and composer with his own bands *The Kids* and *Six Gun Method*, began to practise some of the musical numbers in between shooting scenes off the Florida coast in 2006 for the two *Pirates of the Caribbean* movies – *Dead Man's Chest* and *At The World's End*. Back on dry land he took more singing lessons with his partner, Vanessa Paradis. He was also involved in creating the 'look' of the screen's latest Sweeney Todd – a large 'blaze' or quiff of white hair amidst his long black locks to match the demon barber's pasty face.

A list of notable British actors and actresses co-starred with Depp, including Helena Bonham Carter playing Mrs.Lovett, Alan Rickman as Judge Turpin, Timothy Spall as Beadle Bamford and the impressionist Sacha Baron Cohen as Signor Adolfo Pirelli. Jayne Wisener and Ed Sanders played the young lovers, Johanna and Tobias Ragg. Plans for the two voices of Sweeney's conscience, Anthony Head and Peter Bowles 'The Ballad Ghosts,' to be augmented by Christopher Lee as the 'Gentleman Ghost' were apparently dropped from the film.

Publicity and posters for the film before its release proclaimed, 'Johnny Depp *is* . . . Sweeney Todd' and this re-emphasised one fact for me yet again. The man who apparently never was – it seems – still possesses after all these years the notoriety, the charisma and above all the sense of *mystery* about him, to appeal to each succeeding generation.

PETER HAINING
September 2007

Appendix 1

The Monster of Scotland

Sawney Beane was born in the county of East Lothian, about eight miles east of Edinburgh, in the reign of James VI. His father was a hedger and ditcher, and brought up his son to the same laborious employment. Naturally idle and vicious, he abandoned that place, along with a young woman equally idle and profligate, and they retired to the deserts of Galloway, and took up their habitation by the sea side. The place which Sawney and his wife selected for their dwelling, was a cave of about a mile in length, and of considerable breadth; so near the sea that the tide often penetrated into the cave above two hundred yards. The entry had many intricate windings and turnings which led to the extremity of the subterraneous dwelling, which was literally 'the habitation of horrid cruelty.'

Sawney and his wife took shelter in this cave and commenced their depredations. To prevent the possibility of detection, they murdered every person that they robbed. Destitute also of the means of obtaining any other food, they resolved to live upon human flesh. Accordingly, when they had murdered any man, woman, or child, they carried them to their den, quartered them, salted and pickled the members, and dried them for food. In this manner they lived, carrying on their depredations and murder, until they had eight sons and six daughters, eighteen grandsons and fourteen grand-daughters, all the offspring of incest.

But, though they soon became numerous; yet, such was the multitude who fell into their hands, that they had often superabundance of provisions, and would, at a distance from their own habitation, throw legs and arms of dried human bodies into the sea by night. These were often thrown out by the tide, and taken up by the country people, to the great consternation and dismay of all the surrounding inhabitants. Nor could any discover what had befallen the many friends, relations, and neighbours who had unfortunately fallen into the hands of these merciless cannibals.

In proportion as Sawney's family increased, every one that was able, acted his part in their horrid assassinations. They would sometimes attack four or six men on foot, but never more than two upon horseback. To prevent the possibility of escape, they would lay an ambush in every direction, that if they escaped those who first attacked, they might be assailed with renewed iury by another party, and inevitably murdered. By this means, they always secured their prey and prevented detection.

At last, however, the vast number who were slain, raised the inhabitants of the country, and all the woods and lurking places were carefully searched; and though they often passed by the mouth of the horrible den, it was never once suspected that any human being resided there. In this state of uncertainty and suspense, concerning the authors of such frequent massacres, several innocent travellers and innkeepers were taken up upon suspicion; because, the persons who were missing, had been seen last in their company, or had last resided at their houses. The effect of this well-meant and severe justice, constrained the greater part of the inn-keepers in these parts, to abandon such employments, to the great inconvenience of those who travelled through that district.

Meanwhile, the country became depopulated, and the whole nation was surprised, how such numerous and unheard-of villainies and cruelties could be perpetrated, without the least discovery of the abominable actors. At length, Providence interposed in the following manner to terminate the horrid scene. One evening, a man and his wife were riding home upon the same horse from a fair which had been held in the neighbourhood; and being attacked, he made the most vigorous resistance; unfortunately, however, his wife was dragged from behind him, carried to a little distance, and her entrails instantly taken out. Struck with grief and horror, the husband continued to redouble his efforts to escape, and even trod some of them under his horse's feet. Fortunately for him, and for the inhabitants of that part of the country, in the meantime, twenty or thirty in a company came riding home from the same fair. Upon their approach, Sawney and his bloody crew fled into a thick wood, and hastened to their infernal den.

This man, who was the first that had ever escaped out of their hands, related to his neighbours what had happened, and shewed them the mangled body of his wife, which lay at a distance, the blood-thirsty wretches not having time to carry it along with them. They were all struck with astonishment and horror, took him with them to Glasgow, and reported the whole adventure to the chief magistrate of the city. Upon this intelligence, he wrote to the king, informing him of the matter.

In a few days, his majesty in person, accompanied by four hundred men, went in quest of the perpetrators of such cruelties: the man who had his wife murdered before his eyes, went as their guide, with a great number of blood-hounds, that no possible means might be left unattempted to discover the haunts of these execrable villains.

They searched the woods, traversed and examined the sea-shore; but though they passed by the entrance of their cave, they had no suspicion that any creature resided in that dark and dismal abode. Fortunately, however, some of the blood-hounds entered the cave, raised up an uncommon barking and noise, indicating that they were about to seize their prey. The king and his men returned, but could scarcely conceive how any human being could reside in a place of utter darkness, and where the entrance was difficult and narrow, but as the blood-hounds increased in their vociferation, and refused to return, it occured to all that the cave ought to be explored to the extremity. Accordingly a sufficient number of torches were provided. The hounds were permitted to pursue their course; a great number of men penetrated through all the intricacies of the path, and at length arrived at the private residence of these horrible cannibals.

They were followed by all the band, who were shocked to behold a sight unequalled in Scotland, if not in any part of the universe. Legs, arms, thighs, hands, and feet, of men, woman, and children, were suspended in rows like dried beef. Some limbs and other members were soaked in pickle; while a great mass of money, both of gold and silver, watches, rings, pistols, cloths, both woollen and linen, with an inconceivable quantity of other articles, were either thrown together in heaps, or suspended on the sides of the cave.

The whole cruel brutal family, to the number formerly mentioned, were seized; the human flesh buried in the sand of the sea-shore : the immense booty carried away, and the king marched to Edinburgh with the prisoners. This new and wretched spectacle attracted the attention of the inhabitants, who flocked from all quarters to see this bloody and unnatural family as they passed along, which had increased, in the space of twenty-five years, to the number of twenty-seven men, and twenty-one women. Arrived in the capital, they were all confined in the Tolbooth under a strong guard; they were next day conducted to the common place of execution in Leith Walk, and executed without any formal trial, it being deemed unnecessary to try those who were avowed enemies to all mankind, and of all social order.

The enormity of their crimes dictated the severity of their death. The men had their privy-members thrown into the fire, their hands and legs were severed from their bodies, and they were permitted to bleed to death. The wretched mother of the whole crew, the daughters and grand-children, after being spectators of the death of the men, were cast into three separate fires, and consumed to ashes. Nor did they, in general, display any signs of repentance or regret, but continued with their last breath, to pour forth the most dreadful curses and imprecations upon all around, and upon all those who were instrumental in bringing them to such well-merited punishment.

Appendix 2

Horrible Murder and Human Pie Maker

In the Rue-de-la-Harpe, which is a long dismal ancient street in the Faubourg of St Marcell, is a space or gap in the line of buildings upon which formerly stood two dwelling-houses, instead of which stands now a melancholy memorial, signifying, that upon this spot no human habitation shall ever be erected, no human being ever must reside!

Curiosity will, of course, be greatly excited to ascertain what it was that rendered this devoted spot so obnoxious to humanity, and yet so interesting to history.

Two attached and opulent neighbours, residing in some province, not very remote from the French capital, having occasion to go to town on certain money transactions, agreed to travel thence and to return together, which was to be done with as much expedition as possible. They were on foot, a very common way even at present, for persons of much respectability to travel in France, and were attended, as most pedestrians are, by a faithful dog.

Upon their arrival at the Rue-de-la-Harpe, they stepped into the shop of a peruquier to be shaved, before they would proceed to business, or enter into the more fashionable streets. So limited was their time, and peremptory was their return, that the first man who was shaved, proposed to his companion, that while he was undergoing the operation of the razor, he who was already shaved would run and execute a small commission in the neighbourhood, promising that he would be back before the other was ready to move. For this purpose he left the shop of the barber.

On returning, to his great surprise and vexation, he was informed that his friend was gone; but as the dog, which was the dog of the absentee, was sitting outside of the door, the other presumed he was only gone out for the moment, perhaps in pursuit of him; so expecting him back every moment, he chatted to the barber whilst he waited his return.

Such a considerable time elapsed that the stranger now became quite impatient, he went in and out, up and down the street, still the dog remained stationed at the door. 'Did he leave no message?' 'No'; all the barber knew was that when he was shaved he went away. It certainly was very odd.

The dog remaining stationed at the door was to the traveller conclusive evidence that his master was not far off; he went in and out, up and down the street again. Still no signs of him whatever.

Impatience now became alarm; alarm became sympathetic,. The poor animal exhibited marks of restlessness in yelps and in howlings, which so affected the sensibility of the stranger, that he threw out some insinuations not much to the credit of the barber, who indignantly ordered him to quit his boutique.

Upon quitting the shop he found it impossible to remove the dog from the door. No whistling, no calling, no patting would do, stir he would not.

In his agony, the afflicted man raised a crowd about the door, to whom he told his lamentable story. The dog became an object of universal interest, and of close attention. He shivered and he howled, but no seduction, no caressing, no experiment, could make him desert his post.

By some of the populace it was proposed to send for the police, by others it was proposed a remedy more summary, namely to force in and search the house, which was immediately done. The crowd burst in, every apartment was searched, but in vain. There was no trace whatever of the countryman.

During this investigation, the dog still remained sentinel at the shop-door, which was bolted within to keep out the crowd, which was immense outside.

After a fruitless search and much altercation, the barber, who had prevailed upon those who had forced in to quit his house, came to the door, and was haranguing the populace, declaring most solemnly his innocence, when the dog suddenly sprang upon him, flew at his throat in such a state of terrific exasperation, that his victim fainted, and was with the utmost difficulty rescued from being torn to pieces. The dog seemed to be in a state of intellectual agony and fury.

It was now proposed to give the animal his way, to see what course he would pursue. The moment he was let loose, he flew through the shop, darted down-stairs into a dark cellar, where he set up the most dismal howlings and lamentations.

Lights being procured, an aperture was discovered in the wall communicating to the next house, which was immediately surrounded, in the cellar whereof was found the body of the unfortunate man who had been missing. The person who kept this shop was a patissier.

It is unnecessary to say that those miscreants were brought to trial and executed. The facts that appeared upon their trial, and afterwards upon confession, were these:

Those incautious travellers, whilst in the shop of this fiend, unhappily talked of the money they had about them, and the wretch, who was a robber and murderer by profession, as soon as the one turned his back, drew his razor across the throat of the other and plundered him.

The remainder of the story is almost too horrible for human ears, but is not upon that account the less credible.

The pastry-cook, whose shop was so remarkable for savory patties that they were sent for to the Rue-de-la-Harpe, from the most distant parts of Paris, was the partner of this peruquier, and those who were murdered by the razor of the one were concealed by the knife of the other in those very identical patties, by which, independently of his partnership in those frequent robbers, he had made a fortune.

This case was of so terrific a nature, it was made part of the sentence of the law, that besides the execution of the monsters upon the rack, the houses in which they perpetrated those infernal deeds, should be pulled down, and that the spot on which they stood should be marked out to posterity with horror and execration.

Appendix 3

The Murderous Barber of Calais

I will relate a story which happened in Calais concerning an affair between a barber and a pie-maker which took place thus. The barber had a front chamber in his house in front of his own room. Below that chamber-floor he had made for himself a secret cellar and above the floor was a square trap-door, so nicely made that one who did not look for it closely could not see where it was joined, and the said trap-door shut so hard that a person could sit on a chair on it and it did not go down by it. But when one stamped once hard on it with the foot, it fell down immediately.

Now when any traveller who was of a foreign nation came to this barber to be shaved, then he took him into this said chamber, placed a chair on the aforesaid trap door for him to sit upon while he was to shave him. The stranger did thus. When now the barber began to shave him and came to shave him under the chin, he cut his throat, stamped thus while he cut him and the said trap-door with his foot, by which the trap door with the man and chair fell down into the cellar and immediately thereafter he robbed him. And because the said barber and a pie-maker were in company and council together in this affair, the former sold the human flesh to the latter with which he baked the delicious, palatable and rare pies which were widely sold.

These two were at last discovered and betrayed in this manner, namely. Two travelling students from a foreign country arrived there, and in going along the street came right before the barber's house. Then one companion said to the other, 'Brother, go and engage good lodgings for us somewhere, where you can find some good people. I will, in the meantime, go into this barber to get shaved, where I will wait for you until you return to me here again.' However, the barber did away with him, after his usual aforesaid manner and custom with others.

Now finally the other student returned and asked the barber after his companion. He answered that he went away immediately after he had been shaved. But this companion of his did not believe it, rather considering his companion's word to be more creditable, upon which he relied, but did not know what he should do. Nor would he risk accusing this barber right away, although he had his suspicions, but went away and about the city sought for his companion, but did not find him. He therefore went back to the same barber again and began to quarrel with him, telling him that he must produced his companion, 'For here in this house I must have him again.'

At this, the barber waxed angry and wanted to treat him with striking and beating. The student then made a complaint before a magistrate of the city, stating the nature of the case concerning his comrade, with the request that he might get some good men to go with him to search the barber's house for his companion, which was granted him.

When those arrived who were ordered to search the barber's house, they searched everywhere but could not find him. Finally, they came into the said chamber, where the sergeant stepped on the trap door, saying in an angry tone, 'According to the word and account of this comrade of his, we must really find the man here in the house.' And with this, he stamped on the trap door. Thereby the sergeant fell down into the cellar on the comrade of the other, who had not yet been undressed. Here the cellar was as full of skulls and skeletons as a charnel house in a churchyard.

Thus both the barber and the pie-baker were arrested and locked up and soon afterwards received as a reward a miserable departure from this life. This account is written with the object of instructing him who intends to travel and gain experience, in the first place that he may here from be able to see how very necessary it is for him to have a good and faithful companion and, secondly, that he may know how to guard himself against such villains in similar and in other cases.

Bibliography

Ackroyd, Peter *Evil London: The Dark Side of a City* (Wolfe Publishing, 1973).
  London: The Biography (Chatto & Windus, 2000).
Allen, Thomas *The Histories & Antiquities of London* (Cowie & Strange, 1827).
Altick, Richard D. *The Shows of London* (Harvard University Press, 1978).
  Victorian Studies in Scarlet (J.M.Dent & Sons, 1972).
Bayne-Powell, Rosamond *Eighteenth Century London Life* (John Murray, 1937).
Bell, Walter George *Fleet Street in Seven Centuries* (Isaac Pitman, 1912).
  Unknown London (John Lane, 1919).
Besant, Sir Walter *London in the Eighteenth Century* (Adam & Charles Black, 1902).
  London North of the Thames (Adam & Charles Black, 1911).
Blake, H. Barton *Stories of the Streets of London* (Chapman & Hall, 1899).
Bond, C.G. *Sweeney Todd: A Melodrama* (Samuel French, 1974).
Burke, Thomas *The Streets of London* (B.T.Batsford, 1940).
Burton, Brian J. *Sweeney Todd The Barber* (Combridge Jackson Ltd., 1962).
Cairns, J. A.R. *The Sidelights of London* (Hutchinson, 1924).
Chancellor, E Beresford *Annals of Fleet Street* (Chapman & Hall, 1912).
  The Eighteenth Century in London (B.T.Batsford, 1920).
  Lost London (Constable & Co, 1926).
  Disher, Maurice Wilson *Blood and Thunder* (Frederick Muller Ltd, 1949).
Ditchfield, P.H. *London Survivals* (Methuen & Co, 1914).

Egan, Pierce *Life in London* (Sherwood, Neely & Jones, 1821).

Erie, Thomas W. *Letters From A Theatrical Scene Painter* (Bentley, 1880).

George, Dorothy *London Life in the 18th Century* (Kegan, Paul & Trench, 1930).

Harrison, E. *The New Newgate Calendar* (Harrison, 1864).

Hessels, J.H. *Ecclesiae Londino* (Cambridge, 1887).

Heppenstall, Rayner *Reflections on the Newgate Calendar* (W.H.Allen, 1975).

Hibbert, Christopher *London: The Biography of a City* (Longmans, 1969).

Hobhouse, Hermoine *Lost London* (Macmillan, 1971).

Hughson, David *History of London* (W.Nicoll, 1806).

James, Elizabeth & Smith, Helen R. *Penny Dreadfuls & Boys's Adventures* (British Library, 1998).

James, Louis *Fiction for the Working Man* (Oxford University Press, 1963).

Kent, William *London in the News* (Staples Press, 1954).
London Mystery and Mythology (Staples Press, 1952).

Kilgariff, Michael *The Golden Age of Melodrama* (Wolfe Publishing, 1974).

Knight, Charles (Ed) *London* (Charles Knight & Co, 1841).

Lofts, W.O.G. & Adley, D.J. *The Men Behind Boy's Fiction* (Howard Baker, 1970).

Loftie, W.J. *London City: It's History, Streets & People* (Leadenhall Press, 1891).

Maskell, H.W. *The Crimes of London* (T.Fisher Unwin, 1876).

Medcraft, John *Biography of the Penny Bloods of Edward Lloyd* (Dundee, 1945).

Morris, O. J. *Grandfather's London* (Putnam, 1956).

Nelson, *Thomas Memories of Old London* (Duckworth, 1904).

Newton, H Chance *Crime and the Drama* (Stanley Paul, 1927).

Porter, Roy *London: A Social History* (Hamish Hamilton, 1994).

Prest, Thomas *Newgate* (E. Lloyd, 1847).

Price, F.G. Hilton *The Marygold by Temple Bar* (Bernard Quaritch, 1902).

Rosser, Austin *Sweeney Todd* (Samuel French, 1971).

Scott, *Clement The Drama of Yesterday* (Murray, 1899).

Smith, Helen R. *New Light on Sweeney Todd* (Jarndyce, 2002).

Smith, John Thomas *Ancient Topography of London* (Richard Bentley, 1810).

Sondheim, Stephen & Wheeler, Hugh *Sweeney Todd* (Nick Hern, 1991).

Summers, Montague *A Gothic Bibliography* (Fortune Press, 1940). *The Gothic Quest* (Fortune Press, 1938).

Thornbury, Walter *Haunted London* (Chatto & Windus, 1880). *Old & New London* (Cassell, Potter & Galpin, 1873).

Tillotson, Kathleen *Novels of the Eighteen Forties* (Oxford University Press, 1954).

Turner, E.S. *Boys Will Be Boys* (Michael Joseph, 1948).

Welch, Charles *Modern History of the City of London* (Blades & East, 1896).

Wilkinson, George T. *The Newgate Calendar Improved* (Harrison, 1816).

Williams, E. *Early Holborn* (Sweet & Maxwell, 1927).

Acknowledgements

This book is the result of my own research over many years. However, I have been greatly helped by a number of people who have shared my enthusiasm for getting to the truth about Sweeney Todd. My particular thanks are due to three men who became my friends during the writing of the book, but are sadly no longer alive to share in this new edition: W.O.G. 'Bill' Lofts, David Philips and Ken Chapman. Others who have been generous with their time and knowledge in helping to solve the mystery of the Demon Barber include Alan Dent, Basil Copper, Denis Gifford, Bill Bray, Steve Holland, Jean-Claude Michel, Phyllis Harris, Roy Farrell, Ivy Bass, Alan Pennie, Jeffrey Bloomfield and Anne Williams. Raymond Mander and Joe Mitchenson helped with information from their theatrical museum.

I am also grateful to the staffs of the following libraries that were always patient and helpful in answering my queries on this most elusive of serial killers: The British Museum, The British Newspaper Library at Colindale and the London Library. A number of newspaper publishers have allowed me to quote from their columns, in particular *The Times, The Observer, The Independent, Daily Mail, The Guardian, Time, Variety, Comic Buyer's Guide* and *Notes & Queries* 1849 et al. Much useful information was also obtained from the pages of several defunct publications, including *Strand Magazine, Story Paper Collector* and *The Roundup*.

The illustrations in the book are mostly from my own archives, but the British Film Institute, ABC TV, BBC and the Showtime Network kindly provided a few additional photographs.

Index